VOICES

A Selection of Multicultural Readings

Kathleen S. Verderber
Northern Kentucky University

Wadsworth Publishing Company
I(T)P™ An International Thomson Publishing Company

Belmont • Albany • Bonn • Boston • Cincinnati • Detroit • London • Madrid • Melbourne
Mexico City • New York • Paris • San Francisco • Singapore • Tokyo • Toronto • Washington

For more information, contact:
Wadsworth Publishing Company
10 Davis Drive
Belmont, California 94002 USA

International Thomson Publishing Europe
Berkshire House 168-173
High Holborn
London, WC1V 7AA England

Thomas Nelson Australia
102 Dodds Street
South Melbourne 3205
Victoria, Australia

Nelson Canada
1120 Birchmount Road
Scarborough, Ontario
Canada M1K 5G4

International Thomson Editores
Campos Eliseos 385, Piso 7
Col. Polanco
11560 México D.F. México

International Thomson Publishing GmbH
Königswinterer Strasse 418
53227 Bonn, Germany

International Thomson Publishing Asia
221 Henderson Road
#05-10 Henderson Building
Singapore 0315

International Thomson Publishing Japan
Hirakawacho Kyowa Building, 3F
2-2-1 Hirakawacho
Chiyoda-ku, Tokyo 102 Japan

ISBN 0-534-19563-6

To my parents John and Louise Sheldon, who did not teach me my limitations but rather raised me with the consistent message that I could do anything I set my mind to do, and who sacrificed to support me in those efforts.

Contents

INTRODUCTION

WE WEAR THE MASK

We wear the mask that grins and lies.
It hides our cheeks and shades our eyes,—
This debt we pay to human guile;
With torn and bleeding hearts we smile,
And mouth with myriad subtleties.

Why should the world be over-wise,
In counting all our tears and sighs?
Nay, let them only see us, while
    We wear the mask.

We smile, but, O great Christ, our cries
To thee from tortured souls arise.
We sing, but oh the clay is vile
Beneath our feet, and long the mile;
But let the world dream otherwise,
    We wear the mask!

  Paul Laurence Dunbar

Dunbar is one of America's great poets. His work focused on black folk themes and Southern life. In this poem, which he wrote at the turn of this century, he captures the frustration, pain, and anger of people who must suppress their cultural identities and hide their true feelings. Although writing as a black man, Dunbar expresses sentiments that capture the feelings and experiences of vast numbers of Americans. We who live in the United States of America hold to the ideal that this is the "land of opportunity" and a place where "all men are created equal," while simultaneously knowing that it is also a land of hypocrisy, where people are afforded unequal treatment and opportunity based on their race, sex, religion, class, ability, country of origin, or sexual orientation. Indeed, it is because we as a country hold such high ideals that you, the people who will shape our country's future, must be willing to "step out of your box," your comfort zone, and expose yourselves to viewpoints and realities that are different from your own.

Each time we have revised our textbook *Inter-Act: Using Interpersonal Communication Skills*, Rudy and I have been increasingly aware of how the cultural diversity of our country makes simplistic prescriptions about interpersonal

---

From *The Human Condition: A Rhetoric with Thematic Readings*, eds. Joan Young Gregg and Beth M. Pierce (Belmont, CA: Wadsworth, Inc., 1989), 43.

communication problematic and how our own cultural perspectives limit our viewpoints on these issues. With each edition we have tried to learn and to give more attention to how cultural groups differ in their communication behaviors. Doing this has presented many challenges and although reviewers seem satisfied, we have not been convinced that we were successful in adequately addressing the most salient issues. In part this is because we are increasingly sensitive to the cultural blinders of our white, well-educated, upper-middle class, middle-aged, midwestern, married with children, heterosexual, Christian, European-American perspective. When we write, no matter how much we read and how sensitive we try to be, our writings will continue to be informed by these perspectives.

So the short book of readings that you are now holding is our way of giving "voice" to other persons, ideas, and perspectives that we believe will help you to become better communicators. Each of these previously published articles offers important insights into interpersonal communication processes. Each of the articles will expand your understanding of the richness in interpretations and expressions that is part of interpersonal communication.

Some articles in this collection are primarily informative and are based on empirical or qualitative research findings. Although these articles are written impersonally, they help the reader understand how certain communication behaviors, patterns, and practices both define and differentiate cultural groups in the United States. The information provided by these authors can help you to understand and better relate to one another. It may also help you to prevent or more quickly resolve conflicts that might otherwise ensue. For example, in the article "Monochronic and Polychronic Time," Edward T. Hall discusses two distinct cultural orientations to time. Without this awareness to provide a context for understanding behavior, it is easy for people who have been shaped by different time systems to experience each other as "inappropriate," "rude," and so on, instead of just different.

Other articles, though describing important interpersonal communication characteristics, are more personal, and the author's "voice" is more clearly heard. In these articles, the authors' theoretical points are informed by their personal experiences. These articles provide a different sort of learning about diversity and interpersonal communication processes. As such they help illustrate important communication lessons by providing opportunities for us to empathize with the communication experiences of the person whose voice is being heard in the article. When you read Sucheng Chan's article, "You're Short, Besides!" or Karen K. Russell's article, "Growing Up with Privilege and Prejudice," you will have the opportunity to "listen to" and feel the sting of the words visited upon two women because of their "differences." You will have the opportunity to reflect on how such interactions can affect recipients for long periods of time. In short, you will have the opportunity to experience vicariously the reality in which each of these authors lives and to reflect on the extent to which you have exhibited or been a recipient of communication behaviors such as those discussed by these authors.

After each article you will find one or two questions that are designed to help you think about the ideas and issues addressed in the article. You may use these questions as the springboard for entries in a journal, as topics for a short reaction paper, or as a means of mentally preparing for a class discussion.

In college courses where the articles from this Reader are used for class discussion, you will have a special and exciting challenge. In all likelihood you will have classmates who see the world differently from you. As a result the classroom discussions are likely to be lively and heated. This is good! These discussions will provide an excellent forum for you to practice the communication skills that are the heart of your textbook and to participate in stimulating discussions about diversity. But you will only benefit from these readings and discussions if you exert special effort. Unfortunately what sometimes happens when controversial ideas are discussed is "rehearsal" or "tuning out." Rehearsal occurs when you become so busy preparing your next comments that you do not really listen to the comments of others. Tuning out occurs when you seek to avoid information that does not fit your preconceived notions by day dreaming, sleeping, or engaging in other activities not related to listening to the speaker. If you become uncomfortable with some of the articles that you read or some of the ideas expressed by your classmates, that's O.K., that's what getting out of your "box" is all about. Your challenge will be to use the skills of listening, paraphrasing, describing behavior, describing feelings, and being supportive to facilitate the sharing of meanings during these discussions.

In a volume as short as this, I found it impossible to select articles that give voice to all of the rich, diverse subcultures that constitute the United States or to include articles that address all of the salient issues. The articles I have selected are only representative of those that have been written about diversity and communication processes. Luckily, there are many fine anthologies now available that do address a greater variety of issues. It is my hope that through reading the articles in this book and discussing them with your classmates you will be motivated to continue your study of these issues. If each of us is willing to exert effort to learn about the reality of diverse others, we will be better prepared to communicate our meanings effectively and understand the meanings communicated to us. As this happens, we will undoubtedly be better able to respond creatively to the challenges that face our nation.

SELECTION ONE

In this reading Arturo Madrid sets the tone for the readings that are to follow in this volume. At the time this speech was originally delivered, Madrid, who was trained as an analyst of literary texts, served as President of the Tomas Rivera Center, a national institute for policy studies on Hispanic issues. In the speech he describes the conflicting experiences of those who see themselves as different from what has stereotypically been described as "American." Experiencing oneself and being perceived as "other" and experiencing oneself and being perceived as "invisible" are powerful determinants of one's self-concept and form a very special filter through which one communicates with others. In the article, the author also debunks the myth that "quality" must be associated with homogeneity and by definition limited in quantity. Rather, he argues, quality exists in many diverse forms and is demonstrated by people regardless of their cultural group. It is by recognizing the strength in the diverse forms of quality that exist here that we as a nation will be able to forge a better future for all of our citizens.

Diversity and Its Discontents

Arturo Madrid

My name is Arturo Madrid. I am a citizen of the United States, as are my parents and as were my grandparents, and my great-grandparents. My ancestors' presence in what is now the United States antedates Plymouth Rock, even without taking into account any American Indian heritage I might have.

I do not, however, fit those mental sets that define America and Americans. My physical appearance, my speech patterns, my name, my profession (a professor of Spanish) create a text that confuses the reader. My normal experience is to be asked: And where are YOU from?

From *Intercultural Communication: A Reader,* 7th ed., eds. Larry A. Samovar and Richard E. Porter (Belmont, CA: Wadsworth, Inc., 1994), 127–131. Reprinted by permission of *Black Issues in Higher Education.*

My response depends on my mood. Passive-aggressive I answer: "From here." Aggressive-passive I ask: "Do you mean where am I originally from?" But ultimately my answer to those follow-up questions that will ask about origins will be that we have always been from here.

Overcoming my resentment I will try to educate, knowing that nine times out of ten my words fall on inattentive ears. I have spent most of my adult life explaining who I am not.

I am, however, very clearly the *other*, if only your everyday, garden-variety, domestic *other*. I've always known that I was the *other*, even before I knew the vocabulary or understood the significance of otherness.

I grew up in an isolated and historically marginal part of the United States, a small mountain village in the state of New Mexico, the eldest child of parents native to that region and whose ancestors had always lived there. In those vast and empty spaces people who look like me, speak as I do, and have names like mine predominate. But the *americanos* lived among us: the descendants of those nineteenth century immigrants who dispossessed us of our lands; missionaries who came to convert us and stayed to live among us; artists who became enchanted with our land and humanscape; refugees from unhealthy climes, crowded spaces, unpleasant circumstances; and of course, the inhabitants of Los Alamos. More importantly, however, they—*los americanos*—were omnipresent in newspapers, newsmagazines, books, on radio, in movies and ultimately, on television.

Despite the operating myth of the day, school did not erase my *otherness*. It did try to deny it, and in doing so only accentuated it. To this day what takes place in schools is more socialization than education, but when I was in elementary school and given where I was, socialization was everything. School was where one became an American. Because there was a pervasive and systematic denial by the society that surrounded us that we were Americans. That denial was both explicit and implicit. I remember the implicit denial, our absence from the larger cultural, economic, and social spaces; the one that reminded us constantly that we were the *other*. And school was where we felt it most acutely.

Quite beyond saluting the flag and pledging allegiance to it, becoming American was learning English . . . and its corollary: not speaking Spanish. I do not argue that learning English was not appropriate. On the contrary. Like it or not, and we had no basis to make any judgments on that matter, we were Americans by virtue of having been born Americans, and English was the common language of Americans. And there was a myth, a pervasive myth, to the effect that if we only learned to speak English well and particularly without an accent—we would be welcomed into the American fellowship.

The official English movement folks notwithstanding, the true test was not our speech, but rather our names and our appearance, for we would always have an accent, however perfect our pronunciation, however excellent our enunciation, however divine our diction. That accent would be heard in our pigmentation, our physiognomy, our names. We were, in short, the *other*.

Being the *other* is feeling different; it is awareness of being distinct; it is consciousness of being dissimilar. Otherness results in feeling excluded, closed out, precluded, even disdained and scorned.

Being the *other* involves a contradictory phenomenon. On the one hand being the *other* frequently means being invisible. On the other hand, being the *other* sometimes involves sticking out like a sore thumb. What is she/he doing here?

If one is the *other*, one will inevitably be seen stereotypically; will be defined and limited by mental sets that may not bear much relation to existing realities.

There is sometimes a darker side to otherness as well. The *other* disturbs, disquiets, discomforts. It provokes distrust and suspicion. The *other* frightens, scares.

For some of us being the *other* is only annoying; for others it is debilitating; for still others it is damning. For the majority otherness is permanently sealed by physical appearance. For the rest otherness is betrayed by ways of being, speaking, or of doing.

The first half of my life I spent down-playing the significance and consequences of otherness. The second half has seen me wrestling to understand its complex and deeply ingrained realities; striving to fathom why otherness denies us a voice or visibility or validity in American society and its institutions; struggling to make otherness familiar, reasonable, even normal to my fellow Americans.

Yet I also have experienced another phenomenon; that of being a missing person. Growing up in Northern New Mexico I had only a slight sense of us being missing persons. Hispanos, as we called (and call) ourselves in New Mexico, were very much a part of the fabric of the society and there were Hispano professionals everywhere about me: doctors, lawyers, schoolteachers, and administrators. My people owned businesses, ran organizations, and were both appointed and elected public officials.

My awareness of our absence from the larger institutional life of the society became sharper when I went off to college, but even then it was attenuated by the circumstances of history and geography. The demography of Albuquerque still strongly reflected its historical and cultural origins, despite the influx of Midwesterners and Easterners. Moreover, many of my classmates at the University of New Mexico were Hispanos, and even some of my professors. I thought that would also be true at U.C.L.A., where I began graduate studies in 1960. Los Angeles already had a very large Mexican population, and that population was visible even in and around Westwood and on the campus. But Mexican American students were few and mostly invisible and I do not recall seeing or knowing a single Mexican American (or for that matter Black, Asian, or American Indian) professional on the staff or faculty of that institution during the five years I was there.

Needless to say persons like me were not present in any capacity at Dartmouth College, the site of my first teaching appointment, and of course were not even part of the institutional or individual mindset. I knew then that we—a we that had come to encompass American Indians, Asian Americans, Black Americans, Puerto Ricans, and Women—were truly missing persons in American institutional life

Over the past three decades the *de jure* and *de facto* segregation that have historically characterized American institutions have been under assault. As a consequence minorities and women have become part of American institutional life, and although there are still many areas where we are not to be found, the missing persons phenomenon is not as pervasive as it once was. However, the presence of the *other*, particularly minorities, in institutions and in institutional life is, as we say

in Spanish, *a flor de tierra*: spare plants whose roots do not go deep, a surface phenomenon vulnerable to inclemencies of an economic, or political or social nature.

Some of us entered institutional life through the front door; others through the back door; and still others through side doors. Many, if not most of us, came in through windows, and continue to come in through windows. Of those who entered through the front door, some never made it past the lobby; others were ushered into corners and niches. Those who entered through back and side doors inevitably have remained in back and side rooms. And those who entered through windows found enclosures built around them. For despite the lip service given to the goal of the integration of minorities into institutional life, what has frequently occurred instead is ghettoization, marginalization, isolation.

Not only have the entry points been limited, but in addition the dynamics have been singularly conflictive. Rather than entering institutions more or less passively, minorities have of necessity entered them actively, even aggressively. Rather than taking, they have demanded. Institutional relations have thus been adversarial, infused with specific and generalized tensions.

The nature of the entrance and the nature of the space occupied have greatly influenced the view and attitudes of the majority population within those institutions. All of us are put into the same box; that is, no matter what the individual reality, the assessment of the individual is inevitably conditioned by a perception that is held of the class. Whatever our history, whatever our record, whatever our validations, whatever our accomplishments, by and large we are perceived unidimensionally and dealt with accordingly.

Over the past four decades America's demography has undergone significant changes. Since 1965 the principal demographic growth we have experienced in the United States has been of peoples whose national origins are non-European. This population growth has occurred both through births and through immigration. Conversely, as a consequence of careful tracking by government agencies, we now know that the birth rate of the majority population has decreased.

There are some additional demographic changes which should give us something to think about. Black Americans are now to be found in significant numbers in every major urban center in the nation. Hispanic Americans now number over 15,000,000 persons, and American Indians, heretofore a small and rural population, are increasingly more numerous and urban. The Asian American population, which has historically consisted of small and concentrated communities of Chinese, Filipino, and Japanese Americans, has doubled over the past decade, its complexion changed by the addition of Cambodians, Koreans, Hmongs, Vietnamese, et al.

Thus for the next few decades we will continue to see a growth in the percentage of non-European origin Americans as compared to EuroAmericans. To sum up, we now live in the most demographically diverse nation in the world and one that is growing increasingly more so.

One of my purposes here today is to address the question of whether a goal (quality) and a reality (demographic diversity) present a dilemma to one of the most important of American institutions: higher education.

Quality, according to the Oxford English Dictionary, has multiple meanings. One set defines quality as being an essential character, a distinctive and inherent feature. A second describes it as a degree of excellence, of conformity to standards, as superiority in kind. A third makes reference to social status, particularly to persons of high social status. A fourth talks about quality as being a special or distinguishing attribute, as being a desirable trait. Quality is highly desirable in both principle and practice. We all aspire to it in our own person, in our experiences, and of course we all want to be associated with people and operations of quality.

But let us move away from the various dictionary meanings of the word and to our own sense of what it represents and of how we feel about it. First of all we consider quality to be finite; that is, it is limited with respect to quantity; it has very few manifestations; it is not widely distributed. I have it and you have it, but they don't. We associate quality with homogeneity, with uniformity, with standardization, with order, regularity, neatness. Certainly it's always expensive. We tend to identify it with those who lead, with the rich and the famous. And, when you come right down to it, it's inherent. Either you've got it or you ain't.

Diversity, from the Latin *divertere*, meaning to turn aside, to differ, is the condition of being different or having differences, is an instance of being different. Its companion word, *diverse*, means differing, unlike, distinct; having or capable of having various forms; composed of unlike or distinct elements.

Diversity is lack of standardization, of orderliness, homogeneity. Diversity introduces complications, is difficult to organize, is troublesome to manage, is problematical. The way we use the word gives us away. Something is *too* diverse, is *extremely* diverse. We want a *little* diversity.

When we talk about diversity we are talking about the *other*, whatever that *other* might be: someone of a different gender, race, class, national origin; somebody at a greater or lesser distance from the norm; someone outside the set; someone who doesn't fit into the mental configurations that give our lives order and meaning.

In short, diversity is desirable only in principle, not in practice. Long live diversity, . . . as long as it conforms to my standards, to my mind set, to my view of life, to my sense of order.

The United States, by its very nature, by its very development, is the essence of diversity. It is diverse in its geography, population, institutions, technology, its social, cultural, and intellectual modes. It is a society that at its best does not consider quality to be monolithic in form, finite in quantity, or to reside inherently in class. Quality in our society proceeds in large measure out of the stimulus of diverse modes of thinking and acting;

out of the creativity made possible by the different ways in which we approach things.

One of the principal strengths of our society is its ability to address on a continuing and substantive basis the real economic, political, and social problems that have faced and continue to face us. What makes the United States so attractive to immigrants are the protections and opportunities it offers; what keeps our society together is tolerance for cultural, religious, social, political, and even linguistic difference; what makes us a unique, dynamic, and extraordinary nation are the power and creativity of our diversity.

The true history of the U.S. is the one of struggle against intolerance, against oppression, against xenophobia, against those forces that have prohibited persons from participating in the larger life of the society on the basis of their race, their gender, their religion, their national origin, their linguistic, and cultural background. These phenomena are not only consigned to the past. They remain with us and frequently take on virulent dimensions.

If you believe, as I do, that the well-being of a society is directly related to the degree and extent to which all of its citizens participate in its institutions, then you will have to agree that we have a challenge before us. In view of the extraordinary changes that are taking place in our society we need to take up the struggle again, unpleasant as it is. As educated and educator members of this society we have a special responsibility for assuring that all American institutions, not just our elementary and secondary schools, our juvenile halls, or our jails, reflect the diversity of our society. Not to do so is to risk greater alienation on the part of a growing segment of our society; is to risk increased social tension in an already conflictive world; and, ultimately, is to risk the survival of a range of institutions that for all their defects and deficiencies, provide us the opportunity and the freedom to improve our individual and collective lot.

Let me urge you, as you return to your professional responsibilities and to your personal spaces, to reflect on these two words—quality and diversity—and on the mental sets and behaviors that flow out of them. And let me urge you further to struggle against the notion that quality is finite in quantity, limited in its manifestations, or is restricted by considerations of class, gender, race, or national origin; or that quality manifests itself only in leaders and not in followers, in managers and not in workers; or that it has to be associated with verbal agility or elegance of personal style; or that it cannot be seeded, or nurtured, or developed.

Questions for Reflection

1. Describe an experience that you have had in which you felt *other*.

2. Describe a situation in which you have perceived some part of your cultural heritage as being invisible.

SELECTION TWO

Your textbook discusses the importance of language usage in our message construction and meaning sharing. Since language shapes thoughts and attitudes and is itself shaped by thoughts and attitudes, it logically follows that racist language will lead to racist thoughts and vice versa. In this article Robert B. Moore delineates several aspects of racism in the English language. His analysis serves as a useful reminder that we can either be victims of language or its masters.

Racist Stereotyping in the English Language

Robert B. Moore

Language and Culture

An integral part of any culture is its language. Language not only develops in conjunction with a society's historical, economic and political evolution; it also reflects that society's attitudes and thinking. Language not only *expresses* ideas and concepts but actually *shapes* thought.[1] If one accepts that our dominant white culture is racist, then one would expect our language—an indispensable transmitter of culture—to be racist as well. Whites, as the dominant group, are not subjected to the same abusive characterization by our language that people of color receive. Aspects of racism in the English language that will be discussed in this essay include terminology, symbolism, politics, ethnocentrism, and context.

Before beginning our analysis of racism in language we would like to quote part of a TV film review which shows the connection between language and culture.[2]

Depending on one's culture, one interacts with time in a very distinct fashion. One example which gives some cross-cultural insights into the concept of time is language. In Spanish, a watch is said to "walk." In English the watch "runs." In German the watch "functions." And in French the watch "marches." In the Indian culture of the Southwest, people do not refer to time in this way. The value of the watch is displaced with the value of "what time it's getting to be." Viewing these five cultural perspectives of time, one can see some definite emphasis and values that each culture places on time. For example, a cultural perspective may provide a clue to why the negative stereotype of the slow and lazy Mexican who lives in the "Land of Manana" exists in the Anglo value system where time "flies" the watch "runs" and "time is money."

A Short Play on "Black" and "White" Words

Some may blackly (angrily) accuse me of trying to blacken (defame) the English language, to give it a black eye (a mark of shame) by writing such

From *Race, Class, and Gender: An Anthology*, eds. Margaret L. Anderson and Patricia Hill Collins (Belmont, CA: Wadsworth, Inc., 1992), 317–329. Reprinted by permission of the Council on Interracial Books for Children.

black words (hostile). They may denigrate (to cast aspersions; to darken) me by accusing me of being blackhearted (malevolent), of having a black outlook (pessimistic, dismal) on life, of being a blackguard (scoundrel)—which would certainly be a black mark (detrimental fact) against me. Some may black-brow (scowl at) me and hope that a black cat crosses in front of me because of this black deed. I may become a black sheep (one who causes shame or embarrassment because of deviation from the accepted standards), who will be blackballed (ostracized) by being placed on a blacklist (list of undesirables) in an attempt to blackmail (to force or coerce into a particular action) me to retract my words. But attempts to blackjack (to compel by threat) me will have a Chinaman's chance of success, for I am not a yellow-bellied Indian-giver of words, who will whitewash (cover up or gloss over vices or crimes) a black lie (harmful, inexcusable). I challenge the purity and innocence (white) of the English language. I don't see things in black and white (entirely bad or entirely good) terms, for I am a white man (marked by upright firmness) if there ever was one. However, it would be a black day when I would not "call a spade a spade," even though some will suggest a white man calling the English language racist is like the pot calling the kettle black. While many may be niggardly (grudging, scanty) in their support, others will be honest and decent—and to them I say, that's very white of you (honest, decent).

The preceding is of course a white lie (not intended to cause harm), meant only to illustrate some examples of racist terminology in the English language.

Obvious Bigotry

Perhaps the most obvious aspect of racism in language would be terms like "nigger," "spook," "chink," "spic," etc. While these may be facing increasing social disdain, they certainly are not dead. Large numbers of white Americans continue to utilize these terms. "Chink," "gook," and "slant-eyes" were in common usage among U.S. troops in Vietnam. An NBC nightly news broadcast, in February 1972, reported that the basketball team in Pekin, Illinois, was called the "Pekin Chinks" and noted that even though this had been protested by Chinese Americans, the term continued to be used because it was easy, and meant no harm. Spiro Agnew's widely reported "fat Jap" remark and the "little Jap" comment of lawyer John Wilson, during the Watergate hearings, are surface indicators of a deep-rooted Archie Bunkerism.

Many white people continue to refer to Black people as "colored," as for instance in a July 30, 1975 *Boston Globe* article on a racist attack by whites on a group of Black people using a public beach in Boston. One white person was quoted as follows:

We've always welcomed good colored people in South Boston but we will not tolerate radical blacks or Communists. . . . Good colored people are welcome in South Boston, black militants are not.

Many white people may still be unaware of the disdain many African Americans have for the term "colored," but it often appears that whether used intentionally or unintentionally, "colored" people are "good" and "know their place," while "Black" people are perceived as "uppity" and "threatening" to many whites. Similarly, the term "boy" to refer to African American men is now acknowledged to be a demeaning term, though still in common use. Other terms such as "the pot calling the kettle black" and "calling a spade a spade" have negative racial connotations but are still frequently used, as for example when President Ford was quoted in February 1976 saying that even though Daniel Moynihan had left the U.N., the U.S. would continue "calling a spade a spade."

Color Symbolism

The symbolism of white as positive and black as negative is pervasive in our culture, with the black/white words used in the beginning of this essay only one of many aspects. "Good guys" wear white hats and ride white horses, "bad guys" wear black hats and ride black horses. Angels are white, and devils are black. The definition of *black* includes "without any moral light or goodness, evil, wicked, indicating disgrace, sinful," while that of *white* includes "morally pure, spotless, innocent, free from evil intent."

A children's TV cartoon program, *Captain Scarlet,* is about an organization called Spectrum, whose purpose is to save the world from an evil extraterrestrial force called the Mysterons. Everyone in Spectrum has a color name—Captain Scarlet, Captain Blue, etc. The one Spectrum agent who has been mysteriously taken over by the Mysterons and works to advance their evil aims is Captain Black. The person who heads Spectrum, the good organization out to defend the world, is Colonel White.

Three of the dictionary definitions of white are "fairness of complexion, purity, innocence." These definitions affect the standards of beauty in our culture, in which whiteness represents the norm. "Blondes have more fun" and "Wouldn't you really rather be a blonde" are sexist in their attitudes toward women generally, but are racist white standards when applied to third world women. A 1971 *Mademoiselle* advertisement pictured a curly-headed, ivory-skinned woman over the caption, "When you go blonde go all the way," and asked: "Isn't this how, in the back of your mind, you always wanted to look? All wide-eyed and silky blonde down to there, and innocent?" Whatever the advertising people meant by this particular woman's innocence, one must remember that "innocent" is one of the definitions of the word white. This standard of beauty when preached to all women is racist. The statement "Isn't this how, in the back of your mind, you always wanted to look?" either ignores third world women or assumes they long to be white.

Time magazine in its coverage of the Wimbledon tennis competition between the black Australian Evonne Goolagong and the white American Chris Evert described Ms. Goolagong as "the dusky daughter of an Australian sheepshearer," while Ms. Evert was "a fair young girl from the middle-class groves of Florida." *Dusky* is a synonym of "black" and is defined as "having dark skin; of a dark color; gloomy; dark; swarthy." Its antonyms are "fair" and "blonde." *Fair* is defined in part as "free from blemish, imperfection, or anything that impairs the appearance, quality, or character: pleasing in appearance, attractive; clean; pretty; comely." By defining Evonne Goolagong as "dusky," *Time* technically defined her as the opposite of "pleasing in appearance; attractive; clean; pretty; comely."

The studies of Kenneth B. Clark, Mary Ellen Goodman, Judith Porter and others indicate that this persuasive "rightness of whiteness" in U.S. culture affects children before the age of four, providing white youngsters with a false sense of superiority and encouraging self-hatred among third world youngsters.

Ethnocentrism or from a White Perspective

Some words and phrases that are commonly used represent particular perspectives and frames of reference, and these often distort the understanding of the reader or listener. David R. Burgest[3] has written about the effect of using the terms "slave" or "master." He argues that the psychological impact of the statement referring to "the master raped his slave" is different from the impact of the same statement substituting the words: "the white captor raped an African woman held in captivity."

Implicit in the English usage of the "master-slave" concept is ownership of the "slave" by the "master," therefore, the "master" is merely abusing his property (slave). In reality, the captives (slave) were African individuals with human worth, right and dignity and the term "slave" denounces that human quality thereby making the mass rape of African women by white captors more acceptable in the minds of people and setting a mental frame of reference for legitimizing the atrocities perpetuated against African people.

The term slave connotes a less than human quality and turns the captive person into a thing. For example, two McGraw-Hill Far Eastern Publishers textbooks (1970) stated, "At first it was the slaves who worked the cane and they got only food for it. Now men work cane and get money." Next time you write about slavery or read about it, try transposing all "slaves" into "African people held in captivity," "Black people forced to work for no pay" or "African people stolen from their families and societies." While it is more cumbersome, such phrasing conveys a different meaning.

Passive Tense

Another means by which language shapes our perspective has been noted by Thomas Greenfield,[4] who writes that the achievements of Black people—and Black people themselves—have been hidden in

the linguistic ghetto of the passive voice, the subordinate clause, and the "understood" subject. The seemingly innocuous distinction (between active/passive voice) holds enormous implications for writers and speakers. When it is effectively applied, the rhetorical impact of the passive voice—the art of making the creator or instigator of action totally disappear from a reader's perception—can be devastating.

For instance, some history texts will discuss how European immigrants came to the United States seeking a better life and expanded opportunities, but will note that "slaves *were brought* to America." Not only does this omit the destruction of African societies and families, but it ignores the role of northern merchants and southern slaveholders in the profitable trade in human beings. Other books will state that "the continental railroad *was built*," conveniently omitting information about the Chinese laborers who built much of it or the oppression they suffered.

Another example. While touring Monticello, Greenfield noted that the tour guide

made all the black people of Monticello disappear through her use of the passive voice. While speaking of the architectural achievements of Jefferson in the active voice, she unfailingly shifted to passive when speaking of the work performed by Negro slaves and skilled servants.

Noting a type of door that after 166 years continued to operate without need for repair, Greenfield remarks that the design aspect of the door was much simpler than the actual skill and work involved in building and installing it. Yet his guide stated: "Mr. Jefferson designed these doors . . ." while "the doors were installed in 1809." The workers who installed those doors were African people whom Jefferson held in bondage. The guide's use of the passive tense enabled her to dismiss the reality of Jefferson's slaveholding. It also meant that she did not have to make any mention of the skills of those people held in bondage.

Politics and Terminology

"Culturally deprived," "economically disadvantaged" and "underdeveloped" are other terms which mislead and distort our awareness of reality. The application of the term "culturally deprived" to third world children in this society reflects a value judgment. It assumes that the dominant whites are cultured and all others without culture. In fact, third world children generally are bicultural, and many are bilingual, having grown up in their own culture as well as absorbing the dominant culture. In many ways, they are equipped with skills and experiences which white youth have been deprived of, since most white youth develop in a monocultural, monolingual environment. Burgest[5] suggests that the term "culturally deprived" be replaced by "culturally dispossessed," and that the term "economically disadvantaged" be replaced by "economically exploited." Both these terms present a perspective and implication that provide an entirely different frame of reference as to the reality of the third world experience in U.S. society.

Similarly, many nations of the third world are described as "underdeveloped." These less wealthy nations are generally those that suffered under colonialism and neo-colonialism. The "developed" nations are those that exploited their resources and wealth. Therefore, rather than referring to these countries as "underdeveloped," a more appropriate and meaningful designation might be "over exploited." Again, transpose this term next time you read about "underdeveloped nations" and note the different meaning that results.

Terms such as "culturally deprived," "economically disadvantaged" and "underdeveloped" place the responsibility for their own conditions on those being so described. This is known as "Blaming the Victim."[6] It places responsibility for poverty on the victims of poverty. It removes the blame from those in power who benefit from, and continue to permit, poverty.

Still another example involves the use of "non-white," "minority" or "third world." While people of color are a minority in the U.S., they are part of the vast majority of the world's population, in which white people are a distinct minority. Thus, by utilizing the term minority to describe people of color in the U.S., we can lose sight of the global majority/minority reality—a fact of some importance in the increasing and interconnected struggles of people of color inside and outside the U.S.

To describe people of color as "non-white" is to use whiteness as the standard and norm against which to measure all others. Use of the term "third world" to describe all people of color overcomes the inherent bias of "minority" and "non-white." Moreover, it connects the struggles of third world people in the U.S. with the freedom struggles around the globe.

The term third world gained increasing usage after the 1955 Bandung Conference of "non-aligned" nations, which represented a third force outside of the two world superpowers. The "first world" represents the United States, Western Europe and their sphere of influence. The "second world" represents the Soviet Union and its sphere. The "third world" represents, for the most part, nations that were, or are, controlled by the "first world" or West. For the most part, these are nations of Africa, Asia and Latin America.

"Loaded" Words and Native Americans

Many words lead to a demeaning characterization of groups of people. For instance, Columbus, it is said, "discovered" America. The word *discover* is defined as "to gain sight or knowledge of something previously unseen or unknown; to discover may be to find some existent thing that was previously unknown." Thus, a continent inhabited by millions of human beings cannot be "discovered." For history books to continue this usage represents a Eurocentric (white European) perspective on world history and ignores the existence of, and the perspective of, Native Americans. "Discovery," as used in the Euro-American context, implies the right to take what one finds, ignoring the rights of those who already inhabit or own the "discovered" thing.

Eurocentrism is also apparent in the usage of "victory" and "massacre" to describe the battles between Native Americans and whites. *Victory* is defined in the dictionary as "a success or triumph over an enemy in battle or war; the decisive defeat of an opponent." *Conquest* denotes the "taking over of control by the victor, and the obedience of the conquered." *Massacre* is defined as "the unnecessary, indiscriminate killing of a number of human beings, as in barbarous warfare or persecution, or for revenge or plunder." *Defend* is described as "to ward off attack from; guard against assault or injury; to strive to keep safe by resisting attack."

Eurocentrism turns these definitions around to serve the purpose of distorting history and justifying Euro-American conquest of the Native American homelands. Euro-Americans are not described in history books as invading Native American lands, but rather as defending *their* homes against "Indian" attacks. Since European communities were constantly encroaching on land already occupied, then a more honest interpretation would state that it was the Native Americans who were "warding off," "guarding" and "defending" their homelands.

Native American victories are invariably defined as "massacres," while the indiscriminate killing, extermination and plunder of Native American nations by Euro-Americans is defined as "victory." Distortion of history by the choice of "loaded" words used to describe historical events is a common racist practice. Rather than portraying Native Americans as human beings in highly defined and complex societies, cultures and civilizations, history books use such adjectives as "savages," "beasts," "primitive," and "backward." Native people are referred to as "squaw," "brave," or "papoose" instead of "woman," "man," or "baby."

Another term that has questionable connotations is *tribe*. The Oxford English Dictionary defines this noun as "a race of people; now applied especially to a primary aggregate of people in a primitive or barbarous condition, under a headman or chief." Morton Fried,[7] discussing "The Myth of Tribe," states that the word "did not become a general term of reference to American Indian society until the nineteenth century. Previously, the words commonly used for Indian populations were 'nation' and 'people.' " Since "tribe" has assumed a connotation of primitiveness or backwardness, it is suggested that the use of "nation" or "people" replace the term whenever possible in referring to Native American peoples.

The term *tribe* invokes even more negative implications when used in reference to American peoples. As Evelyn Jones Rich[8] has noted, the term is "almost always used to refer to third world people and it implies a stage of development which is, in short, a put-down."

"Loaded" Words and Africans

Conflicts among diverse peoples within African nations are often referred to as "tribal warfare," while conflicts among the diverse peoples within European countries are never described in such terms. If the rivalries between the Ibo and the Hausa and Yoruba in Nigeria are described as "tribal," why not the rivalries between Serbs and Slavs in Yugoslavia, or Scots and English in Great Britain, Protestants and Catholics in Ireland, or the Basques and the Southern Spaniards in Spain? Conflicts among African peoples in a particular nation have religious, cultural, economic and/or political roots. If we can analyze the roots of conflicts among European peoples in terms other than "tribal warfare," certainly we can do the same with African peoples, including correct reference to the ethnic groups or nations involved. For example, the terms "Kaffirs," "Hottentot" or "Bushmen" are names imposed by white Europeans. The correct names are always those by which a people refer to themselves. (In these instances Xhosa, Khoi-Khoin and San are correct.[9])

The generalized application of "tribal" in reference to Africans—as well as the failure to acknowledge the religious, cultural and social diversity of African peoples—is a decidedly racist dynamic. It is part of the process whereby Euro-Americans justify, or avoid confronting, their oppression of third world peoples. Africa has been particularly insulted by this dynamic, as witness the pervasive "darkest Africa" image. This image, widespread in Western culture, evokes an Africa covered by jungles and inhabited by "uncivilized," "cannibalistic," "pagan," "savage" peoples. This "darkest Africa" image avoids the geographical reality. Less than 20 per cent of the African continent is wooded savanna, for example. The image also ignores the history of African cultures and civilizations. Ample evidence suggests this distortion of reality was developed as a convenient rationale for the European and American slave trade. The Western powers, rather than exploiting, were civilizing and Christianizing "uncivilized" and "pagan savages" (so the rationalization went). This dynamic also served to justify Western colonialism. From Tarzan movies to racist children's books like *Doctor Dolittle* and *Charlie and the Chocolate Factory*, the image of "savage" Africa and the myth of "the white man's burden" has been perpetuated in Western culture.

A 1972 *Time* magazine editorial lamenting the demise of *Life* magazine, stated that the "lavishness" of *Life's* enterprises included "organizing safaris into darkest Africa." The same year, the *New York Times'* C. L. Sulzberger wrote that Africa has "a history as dark as the skins of many of its people." Terms such as "darkest Africa," "primitive," "tribe" ("tribal") or "jungle," in reference to Africa, perpetuate myths and are especially inexcusable in such large circulation publications.

Ethnocentrism is similarly reflected in the term "pagan" to describe traditional religions. A February 1973 *Time* magazine article on Uganda stated, "Moslems account for only 500,000 of Uganda's 10 million people. Of the remainder, 5,000,000 are Christians and the rest pagan." *Pagan* is defined as "Heathen, a follower of a polytheistic religion; one that has little or no religion and that is marked by a frank delight in and uninhibited seeking after sensual pleasures and material goods." *Heathen* is defined as "Unenlightened; an unconverted member of a people or nation that does not acknowledge the God of the Bible. A person whose culture or enlightenment is of an inferior grade, especially an irreligious person." Now, the people of Uganda, like almost all Africans, have serious religious beliefs and practices. As used by Westerners, "pagan" connotes something wild, primitive and inferior—another term to watch out for.

The variety of traditional structures that African people live in are their "houses," not "huts." A hut is "an often small and temporary dwelling of simple construction." And to describe Africans as "natives" (noun) is derogatory terminology—as in, "the natives are restless." The dictionary definition of *native* includes: "one of a people inhabiting a territorial area at the time of its discovery or becoming familiar to a foreigner; one belonging to a people having a less complex civilization." Therefore, use of "native," like use

of "pagan" often implies a value judgment of white superiority.

Qualifying Adjectives

Words that would normally have positive connotations can have entirely different meanings when used in a racial context. For example, C. L. Sulzberger, the columnist of the *New York Times*, wrote in January 1975, about conversations he had with two people in Namibia. One was the white South African administrator of the country and the other a member of SWAPO, the Namibian liberation movement. The first is described as "Dirk Mudge, who as senior elected member of the administration is a kind of acting Prime Minister. . . ." But the second person is introduced as "Daniel Tijongarero, an intelligent Herero tribesman who is a member of SWAPO. . . ." What need was there for Sulzberger to state that Daniel Tijongarero is "intelligent"? Why not also state that Dirk Mudge was "intelligent"—or do we assume he wasn't?

A similar example from a 1968 *New York Times* article reporting on an address by Lyndon Johnson stated, "The President spoke to the well-dressed Negro officials and their wives." In what similar circumstances can one imagine a reporter finding it necessary to note that an audience of white government officials was "well-dressed"?

Still another word often used in a racist context is "qualified." In the 1960's white Americans often questioned whether Black people were "qualified" to hold public office, a question that was never raised (until too late) about white officials like Wallace, Maddox, Nixon, Agnew, Mitchell, et al. The question of qualifications has been raised even more frequently in recent years as white people question whether Black people are "qualified" to be hired for positions in industry and educational institutions. "We're looking for a qualified Black" has been heard again and again as institutions are confronted with affirmative action goals. Why stipulate that Blacks must be "qualified," when for others it is taken for granted that applicants must be "qualified."

Speaking English

Finally, the depiction in movies and children's books of third world people speaking English is often itself racist. Children's books about Puerto Ricans or Chicanos often connect poverty with a failure to speak English or to speak it well, thus blaming the victim and ignoring the racism which affects third world people regardless of their proficiency in English. Asian characters speak a stilted English ("Honorable so and so" or "Confucius say") or have a speech impediment ("roots or ruck," "very solly," "flied lice"). Native American characters speak another variation of stilted English ("Boy not hide. Indian take boy."), repeat certain Hollywood-Indian phrases ("Heap big" and "Many moons") or simply grunt out "Ugh" or "How." The repeated use of these language characterizations functions to make third world people seem less intelligent and less capable than the English-speaking white characters.

Wrap-Up

A *Saturday Review* editorial[10] on "The Environment of Language" stated that language

. . . has as much to do with the philosophical and political conditioning of a society as geography or climate. . . . people in Western cultures do not realize the extent to which their racial attitudes have been conditioned since early childhood by the power of words to ennoble or condemn, augment or detract, glorify or demean. Negative language infects the subconscious of most Western people from the time they first learn to speak. Prejudice is not merely imparted or superimposed. It is metabolized in the bloodstream of society. What is needed is not so much a change in language as an awareness of the power of words to condition attitudes. If we can at least recognize the underpinnings of prejudice, we may be in a position to deal with the effects.

To recognize the racism in language is an important first step. Consciousness of the influence of language on our perceptions can help to negate much of that influence. But it is not enough to simply become aware of the effects of racism in conditioning attitudes. While we may not be able to change the language, we can definitely change our usage of the language. We can avoid using words that degrade people. We can make a conscious effort to use terminology that reflects a progressive perspective, as opposed to a distorting perspective. It is important for educators to provide students with opportunities to explore racism in language and to increase their awareness of it, as well as learning terminology that is positive and does not perpetuate negative human values.

Notes

1. Simon Podair, "How Bigotry Builds Through Language," *Negro Digest*, March '67
2. Jose Armas, "Antonia and the Mayor: A Cultural Review of the Film," *The Journal of Ethnic Studies*, Fall, '75
3. David R. Burgest, "The Racist Use of the English Language," *Black Scholar*, Sept. '73
4. Thomas Greenfield, "Race and Passive Voice at Monticello," *Crisis*, April '75
5. David R. Burgest, "Racism in Everyday Speech and Social Work Jargon," *Social Work*, July '73
6. William Ryan, *Blaming the Victim*, Pantheon Books, '71
7. Morton Fried, "The Myth of Tribe," *National History*, April '75
8. Evelyn Jones Rich, "Mind Your Language," *Africa Report*, Sept./Oct. '74
9. Steve Wolf, "Catalogers in Revolt Against LC's Racist, Sexist Headings," *Bulletin of Interracial Books for Children*, Vol. 6, Nos. 3&4, '75
10. "The Environment of Language," *Saturday Review*, April 8, '67

Also see:

Roger Bastide, "Color, Racism and Christianity," *Daedalus*, Spring '67

Kenneth J. Gergen, "The Significance of Skin Color in Human Relations," *Daedalus*, Spring '67

Lloyd Yabura, "Towards a Language of Humanism,"
   Rhythm, Summer '71

UNESCO, "Recommendations Concerning Terminology in Education on Race Questions," June '68

Questions for Reflection

1. Which types of racist language were you aware of
    prior to reading this article? Which of the new
    categories of racist language seem most problem-
    atic to you?

2. What racist language tendencies are you most
    prone to using? If your immediate answer is none,
    ask a friend or associate who spends a lot of time
    with you to read this article, and then to audit
    your communication for a couple of days and
    report to you the results of his or her
    observations.

3. When others use racist language what do you
    generally do about it? Is your behavior generally
    the same? What is the usual effect of your behav-
    ior on those who have used the racist language, or
    who are also present when it is used? How do you
    feel about the manner in which you choose to
    respond?

SELECTION THREE

In American society, the games that boys have traditionally played and the games that girls have traditionally played have had different goals, rules, and roles. As a result the interaction that is necessary to be successful in each of these distinct speech communities is different. According to Julia T. Wood, Professor of Communication at University of North Carolina Chapel Hill, from childhood men and women are conditioned to have differing communication styles, to talk differently. In this selection from her book *Gendered Lives: Communication, Gender, and Culture*, the origins, behaviors, and motives for each style are discussed. Through understanding both masculine and feminine styles, we should be better equipped to interpret the verbal communication behaviors of both men and women.

Gendered Interaction: Masculine and Feminine Styles of Verbal Communication

Julia T. Wood

Language not only expresses cultural views of gender but also constitutes individuals' gender identities. The communication practices we use define us as masculine or feminine; in large measure, we create our own gender through talk. Because language constitutes masculinity and femininity, we should find generalizable differences in how women and men communicate. Research bears out this expectation by documenting rather systematic differences in the ways men and women typically use language. You probably don't need a textbook to tell you this, since your own interactions may have given you ample evidence of differences in how women and men talk.

What may not be clear from your own experiences, however, is exactly what those differences are and what they imply. If you are like most people, you've sometimes felt uncomfortable or misunderstood or mystified in communication with members of the other sex, but you've not been able to put your finger on what was causing the difficulty. In the pages that follow, we'll try to gain greater insight into masculine and feminine styles of speech and some of the confusion that results from differences between them. We want to understand how each style evolves, what it involves, and how to interpret verbal communication in ways that honor the motives of those using it.

Gendered Speech Communities

Writing in the 1940s, Suzanne Langer introduced the idea of "discourse communities." Like George Herbert Mead, she asserted that culture, or collective life, is possible only to the extent that a group of people share a symbol system and the meanings encapsulated in it. This theme recurred

From *Gendered Lives: Communication, Gender, and Culture*, by Julia T. Wood (Belmont, CA: Wadsworth, Inc., 1994) 137–148. Reprinted by permission of Wadsworth Publishing Company.

in Langer's philosophical writings over the course of her life (1953, 1979). Her germinal insights into discourse communities prefigured later interest in the ways in which language creates individual identity and sustains cultural life. Since the early 1970s, scholars have studied **speech communities**, or cultures. William Labov (1972, p. 121) extended Langer's ideas by defining a speech community as existing when a group of people share a set of norms regarding communicative practices. By this he meant that a communication culture exists when people share understandings about goals of communication, strategies for enacting those goals, and ways of interpreting communication.

It's obvious we have entered a different communication culture when we travel to non-English-speaking countries, because the language differs from our own. Distinct speech communities are less apparent when they use the same language that we do, but use it in different ways and to achieve different goals. The communication culture of African-Americans who have not adopted the dominant pattern of North American speech, for instance, relies on English yet departs in interesting and patterned ways from the communication of middle- class white North Americans. The fact that diverse groups of people develop distinctive communication patterns reminds us again of the constant interaction of communication and culture. As we have already seen, the standpoint we occupy in society influences what we know and how we act. We now see that this basic tenet of standpoint theory also implies that communication styles evolve out of different standpoints.

Studies of gender and communication (Campbell, 1973; Coates, 1986; Coates & Cameron, 1989; Hall & Langellier, 1988; Kramarae, 1981; Lakoff, 1975; Tannen, 1990a, 1990b) have convincingly shown that in many ways women and men operate from dissimilar assumptions about the goals and strategies of communication. F. L. Johnson (1989), in fact, asserts that men and women live in two different worlds and that this is evident in the disparate forms of communication they use. Given this, it seems appropriate to consider masculine and feminine styles of communicating as embodying two distinct speech communities. To understand these different communities and the validity of each, we will first consider how we are socialized into feminine and masculine speech communities. After this, we will explore divergencies in how women and men typically communicate. Please note the importance of the word *typically* and others that indicate we are discussing generalizable differences, not absolute ones. Some women are not socialized into feminine speech, or they are and later reject it; likewise, some men do not learn or choose not to adopt a masculine style of communication. What follows describes gendered speech communities into which *most* women and men are socialized.

The Lessons of Childplay

We've seen that socialization is a gendered process in which boys and girls are encouraged to develop masculine and feminine identities. Extending that understanding, we now explore how socialization creates gendered speech communities. One way to gain insight into how boys and girls learn norms of communication is to observe young children at play. In interactions with peers, boys and girls learn how to talk and how to interpret what each other says; they discover how to signal their intentions with words and how to respond appropriately to others' communication; and they learn codes to demonstrate involvement and interest (Tannen, 1990a). In short, interacting with peers teaches children rules of communication.

Initial insight into the importance of children's play in shaping patterns of communication came from a classic study by D. N. Maltz and R. Borker (1982). As they watched young children engaged in recreation, the researchers were struck by two observations: Young children almost always play in sex-segregated groups, and girls and boys tend to play different kinds of games. Maltz and Borker found that boys' games (football, baseball) and girls' games (school, house, jumprope) cultivate distinct understandings of communication and the rules by which it operates.

Boys' Games

Boys' games usually involve fairly large groups— nine individuals for each baseball team, for instance. Most boys' games are competitive, have clear goals, and are organized by rules and roles that specify who does what and how to play. Because these games are structured by goals, rules, and roles, there is little need to discuss how to play, although there may be talk about strategies to reach goals. Maltz and Borker realized that in boys' games, an individual's status depends on standing out, being better, and often dominating other players. From these games, boys learn how to interact in their communities. Specifically, boys' games cultivate three communication rules:

1. Use communication to assert yourself and your ideas; use talk to achieve something.
2. Use communication to attract and maintain an audience.
3. Use communication to compete with others for the "talk stage," so that they don't gain more attention than you; learn to wrest the focus from others and onto yourself.

These communication rules are consistent with other aspects of masculine socialization that we have already discussed. For instance, notice the emphasis on individuality and competition. Also, we see that these rules accent achievement— doing something, accomplishing a goal. Boys learn they must *do things* to be valued members of the team. It's also the case that intensely close, personal relationships are unlikely to be formed in large groups. Finally, we see the under-

> ## ALAN
>
> I got the message about not letting other guys beat me when I was just 10. Every day on my way home from school, this other boy who was 4 or 5 years older would wait for me so that he could beat on me. I got tired of this, so I talked to my dad about it, hoping he'd help me. But he just lit into me some kind of bad. He told me not to ever, ever come to him again saying some other guy was beating up on me. He told me if that guy came after me again, I should fight back and use something to hit him if I had to.
>
> Sure enough, the next day that dude was waiting for me. When he hit me, I picked up the nearest thing—a two-by-four on the ground—and hit him on the head. Well, he had to go to the hospital, but my dad said that was okay because his son had been a man.

current of masculinity's emphasis on being invulnerable and guarded: If others are the competition from whom you must seize center stage, then you cannot let them know too much about yourself and your weaknesses.

Girls' Games

Turning now to girls' games, we find that quite different patterns exist, and they lead to distinctive understandings of communication. Girls tend to play in pairs or in very small groups rather than large ones. Also, games like house and school do not have preset, clear-cut goals, rules, and roles. There is no analogy for the touchdown in playing house. Because girls' games are not structured externally, players have to talk among themselves to decide what they're doing and what roles they have. Playing house, for instance, typically begins with a discussion about who is going to be the daddy and who the mommy. This is typical of the patterns girls use to generate rules and roles for their games. The lack of stipulated goals for the games is also important, since it tends to cultivate in girls an interest in the process of interaction more than its products. For their games to work, girls have to cooperate and work out problems by talking: No external rules exist to settle disputes. From these games, Maltz and Borker noted, girls learn normative communication patterns of their speech communities. Specifically, girls' games teach three basic rules for communication:

1. Use collaborative, cooperative talk to create and maintain relationships. The *process* of communication, not its content, is the heart of relationships.

2. Avoid criticizing, outdoing, or putting others down; if criticism is necessary, make it gentle; never exclude others.

3. Pay attention to others and to relationships; interpret and respond to others' feelings sensitively.

These basic understandings of communication echo and reinforce other aspects of feminine socialization. Girls' games stress cooperation, collaboration, and sensitivity to others' feelings. Also notice the focus on process encouraged in girls' games. Rather than interacting to achieve some outcome, girls learn that communication itself is the goal. Whereas boys learn they have to do something to be valuable, the lesson for girls is *to be*. Their worth depends on being good people, which is defined by being cooperative, inclusive, and sensitive. The lessons of child's play are carried forward. In fact, the basic rules of communication that adult women and men employ turn out to be only refined and elaborated versions of the very same ones evident in girls' and boys' childhood games.

Gendered Communication Practices

In her popular book, *You Just Don't Understand: Women and Men in Communication*, linguist Deborah Tannen (1990b, p. 42) declares that 'communication between men and women can be like cross cultural communication, prey to a clash of conversational styles." Her study of men's and women's talk led her to identify distinctions between the speech communities typical of women and men. Not surprisingly, Tannen traces gendered communication patterns to differences in boys' and girls' communication with parents and peers. Like other scholars (Bate, 1988; Hall & Langellier, 1988; Kramarae, 1981; Treichler & Kramarae, 1983; Wood, 1993a), Tannen believes that women and men typically engage in distinctive styles of communication with different purposes, rules, and understandings of how to interpret talk. We will consider features of women's and men's speech identified by a number of researchers. As we do, we will discover some of the complications that arise when men and women operate by different rules in conversations with each other.

Women's Speech

For most women, communication is a primary way to establish and maintain relationships with others. They engage in conversation to share themselves and to learn about others. This is an important point: For women, talk *is* the essence of relationships. Consistent with this primary goal, women's speech tends to display identifiable features that foster connections, support, closeness, and understanding.

Equality between people is generally important in women's communication (Aries, 1987). To achieve symmetry, women often match experiences to indicate "You're not alone in how you feel." Typical ways to communicate equality would be saying, "I've done the same thing many times," "I've felt the same way," or "Something like that happened to me too and I felt like you do." Growing out of the quest for equality is a participatory mode of interaction in which communicators respond to and build on each other's ideas in the process of conversing (Hall & Langellier, 1988). Rather than a rigid you-tell-your-ideas-then-I'll-tell-mine sequence, women's speech more characteristically follows an interactive pattern in which different voices weave together to create conversations.

Also important in women's speech is showing support for others. To demonstrate support, women often express understanding and sympathy with a friend's situation or feelings. "Oh, you must feel terrible," "I really hear what you are saying," or "I think you did the right thing" are communicative clues that we understand and support how another feels. Related to these first two features is women's typical attention to the relationship level of communication (Wood, 1993a, 1993b; Wood & Inman, 1993). You will recall that the relationship level of talk focuses on feelings and the relationship between communicators rather than on the content of messages. In conversations between women, it is common to hear a number of questions that probe for greater understanding of feelings and perceptions surrounding the subject of talk (Beck, 1988, p. 104; Tannen, 1990b). "Tell me more about what happened," "How did you feel when it occurred?" "Do you think it was deliberate?" "How does this fit into the overall relationship?" are probes that help a listener understand a speaker's perspective. The content of talk is dealt with, but usually not without serious attention to the feelings involved.

A fourth feature of women's speech style is conversational "maintenance work" (Beck, 1988; Fishman, 1978). This involves efforts to sustain conversation by inviting others to speak and by prompting them to elaborate their experiences.

Women, for instance, ask a number of questions that initiate topics for others: "How was your day?" "Tell me about your meeting," "Did anything interesting happen on your trip?" "What do you think of the candidates this year?" Communication of this sort opens the conversational door to others and maintains interaction.

Inclusivity also surfaces in a fifth quality of women's talk, which is responsiveness (Beck, 1988; Tannen, 1990a, 1990b; Wood, 1993a). Women usually respond in some fashion to what others say. A woman might say "Tell me more" or "That's interesting"; perhaps she will nod and use eye contact to signal she is engaged; perhaps she will ask a question such as "Can you explain what you mean?" Responsiveness reflects learned tendencies to care about others and to make them feel valued and included (Kemper, 1984; Lakoff, 1975). It affirms another person and encourages elaboration by showing interest in what was said.

A sixth quality of women's talk is personal, concrete style (Campbell, 1973; Hall & Langellier, 1988; Tannen, 1990b). Typical of women's conversation are details, personal disclosures, anecdotes, and concrete reasoning. These features cultivate a personal tone in women's communication, and they facilitate feelings of closeness by connecting communicators' lives. The detailed, concrete emphasis prevalent in women's talk also clarifies issues and feelings so that communicators are able to understand and identify with each other. Thus, the personal character of much of women's interaction sustains interpersonal closeness.

A final feature of women's speech is tentativeness. This may be expressed in a number of forms. Sometimes women use verbal hedges such as "I kind of feel you may be overreacting." In other situations they qualify statements by saying "I'm probably not the best judge of this, but . . ." Another way to keep talk provisional is to tag a question onto a statement in a way that invites another to respond: "That was a pretty good movie, wasn't it?" "We should get out this weekend, don't you think?" Tentative communication leaves open the door for others to respond and express their opinions.

There has been controversy about tentativeness in women's speech. R. Lakoff (1975), who first noted that women use more hedges, qualifiers, and tag questions than men, claimed these represent lack of confidence and uncertainty. Calling women's speech powerless, Lakoff argued that it reflects women's socialization into subordinate roles and low self-esteem. Since Lakoff's work, however, other scholars (Bate, 1988; Wood & Lenze, 1991b) have suggested different explanations of women's tentative style of speaking. Dale Spender (1984a), in particular, points out that Lakoff's judgments of the inferiority of women's speech were based on using male speech as the standard, which does not recognize the distinctive validity of different speech communities. Rather than reflecting powerlessness, the use of hedges, qualifiers, and tag questions may express women's desires to keep conversation open and to include others. It is much easier to jump into a conversation that has not been sealed with absolute, firm statements. A tentative style of speaking supports women's general desire to create equality and include others. It is important to realize, however, that people outside of women's speech community may misinterpret women's intentions in using tentative communication.

Men's Speech

Masculine speech communities define the goals of talk as exerting control, preserving independence, and enhancing status. Conversation is an arena for proving oneself and negotiating prestige. This leads to two general tendencies in men's communication. First, men often use talk to establish and defend their personal status and their ideas, by asserting themselves and/or by challenging others. Second, when they wish to comfort or support another, they typically do so by respect-

ing the other's independence and avoiding communication they regard as condescending (Tannen, 1990b). These tendencies will be more clear as we review specific features of masculine talk.

To establish their own status and value, men often speak to exhibit knowledge, skill, or ability. Equally typical is the tendency to avoid disclosing personal information that might make a man appear weak or vulnerable (Derlega & Chaiken, 1976; Lewis & McCarthy, 1988; Saurer & Eisler, 1990). For instance, if someone expresses concern about a relationship with a boyfriend, a man might say "The way you should handle that is . . . ," "Don't let him get to you," or "You ought to just tell him . . ." This illustrates the tendency to give advice that Tannen reports is common in men's speech. On the relationship level of communication, giving advice does two things. First, it focuses on instrumental activity—what another should do or be—and does not acknowledge feelings. Second, it expresses superiority and maintains control. It says "I know what you should do" or "I would know how to handle that." The message may be perceived as implying the speaker is superior to the other person. Between men, advice giving seems understood as a give-and-take, but it may be interpreted as unfeeling and condescending by women whose rules for communicating differ.

A second prominent feature of men's talk is instrumentality—the use of speech to accomplish instrumental objectives. As we have seen, men are socialized to do things, achieve goals (Bellinger & Gleason, 1982). In conversation, this is often expressed through problem-solving efforts that focus on getting information, discovering facts, and suggesting solutions. Again, between men this is usually a comfortable orientation, since both speakers have typically been socialized to value instrumentality. However, conversations between women and men are often derailed by the lack of agreement on what this informational, instrumental focus means. To many women it feels as if men don't care about their feelings. When a man focuses on the content level of meaning after a woman has disclosed a problem, she may feel he is disregarding her emotions and concerns. He, on the other hand, may well be trying to support her in the way that he has learned to show support—suggesting ways to solve the problem.

A third feature of men's communication is conversational dominance. Despite jokes about women's talkativeness, research indicates that in most contexts, men not only hold their own but dominate the conversation. This tendency, although not present in infancy, is evident in preschoolers (Austin, Salehi, & Leffler, 1987). Compared with girls and women, boys and men talk more frequently (Eakins & Eakins, 1976; Thorne & Henley, 1975) and for longer periods of time (Aries, 1987; Eakins & Eakins, 1976; Kramarae, 1981; Thorne & Henley, 1975). Further, men engage in other verbal behaviors that sustain conversational dominance. They may reroute conversations by using what another said as a jump-off point for their own topic, or they may interrupt. While both sexes engage in interruptions, most research suggests that men do it more frequently (Beck, 1988; Mulac, Wiemann, Widenmann, & Gibson, 1988; West & Zimmerman, 1983). Not only do men seem to interrupt more than women, but they do so for different reasons. L. P. Stewart and her colleagues (1990, p. 51) suggest that men use interruptions to control conversation by challenging other speakers or wresting the talk stage from them, while women interrupt to indicate interest and to respond. This interpretation is shared by a number of scholars who note that women use interruptions to show support, encourage elaboration, and affirm others (Aleguire, 1978; Aries, 1987; Mulac et al., 1988).

Fourth, men tend to express themselves in fairly absolute, assertive ways. Compared with women, their language is typically more forceful, direct, and authoritative (Beck, 1988; Eakins & Eakins, 1978; Stewart et al., 1990; Tannen, 1990a, 1990b). Tentative speech such as hedges and disclaimers is used less frequently by men than by women. This is consistent with gender socialization in which men learn to use talk to assert themselves and to take and hold positions. However, when another person does not share that understanding of communication, speech that is absolute and directive may seem to close off conversation and leave no room for others to speak.

Fifth, compared with women, men communicate more abstractly. They frequently speak in general terms that are removed from concrete experiences and distanced from personal feelings (Schaef, 1981; Treichler & Kramarae, 1983). The abstract style typical of men's speech reflects the public and impersonal contexts in which they often operate and the less personal emphasis in their speech communities. Within public environments, norms for speaking call for theoretical, conceptual, and general thought and communication. Yet, within more personal relationships, abstract talk sometimes creates barriers to knowing another intimately.

Finally, men's speech tends not to be highly responsive, especially not on the relationship level of communication (Beck, 1988; Wood, 1993a). Men, more than women, give what are called "minimal response cues" (Parlee, 1979), which are verbalizations such as "yeah" or "umhmm." In interaction with women, who have learned to demonstrate interest more vigorously, minimal response cues generally inhibit conversation because they are perceived as indicating lack of involvement (Fishman, 1978; Stewart et al., 1990). Another way in which men's conversation is generally less relationally responsive than women's is lack of expressed sympathy and understanding and lack of self-disclosures (Saurer & Eisler, 1990). Within the rules of men's speech communities, sympathy is a sign of condescension, and revealing personal problems is seen as making one vulnerable. Yet women's speech rules count sympathy and disclosure as demonstrations of equality and support. This creates potential for misunderstanding between women and men.

Misinterpretations Between Women and Men

In this final section, we explore what happens when men and women talk, each operating out of a distinctive speech community. In describing features typical of each gender's talk, we already have noted differences that provide fertile ground for misunderstandings. We now consider several examples of recurrent misreadings between women and men.

Showing Support

The scene is a private conversation between Martha and George. She tells him she is worried about her friend. George gives a minimum response cue, saying only "Oh." To Martha this suggests he isn't interested, since women make and expect more of what D. Tannen (1986) calls "listening noises" to signal interest. Yet, as Tannen (1986, 1990b) and A. Beck (1988) note, George is probably thinking if she wants to tell him something she will, since his rules of speech emphasize using talk to assert oneself (Bellinger & Gleason, 1982). Even without much encouragement, Martha continues by describing the tension in her friend's marriage and her own concern about how she can help. She says, "I feel so bad for Barbara, and I want to help her, but I don't know what to do." George then says, "It's their problem, not yours. Just butt out and let them settle their own relationship." At this, Martha explodes: "Who asked for your advice?" George is now completely frustrated and confused. He thought Martha wanted advice, so he gave it. She is hurt that George didn't tune into her feelings and comfort her about her worries. Each is annoyed and unhappy.

The problem here is not so much what George and Martha say and don't say. Rather, it's how they interpret each other's communication—actually, how they *misinterpret* it, because each relies on rules that are not familiar to the other. They fail to

---

JAY

Finally I understood this thing that keeps happening between my girlfriend and me. She is always worrying about something or feeling bad about what's happening with one of her friends. I've been trying to be supportive by telling her things like she shouldn't worry, or not to let it get her down, or not to obsess about other people's problems. I was trying to help her feel better. That's what guys do for each other—kind of distract our attention from problems. But Teresa just gets all huffy and angry when I do that. She tells me to stuff my advice and says if I cared about her I would show more concern. Finally, it makes sense. Well, sort of, but I still think the rules she uses are strange.

---

understand that each is operating by different rules of talk. George is respecting Martha's independence by not pushing her to talk. When he thinks she directly requests advice, he offers it in an effort to help. Martha, on the other hand, wants comfort and a connection with George—that is her purpose in talking with him. She finds his advice unwelcome and dismissive of her feelings. He doesn't offer sympathy, because his rules for communication define this as condescending. Yet within Martha's speech community, not to show sympathy is to be unfeeling and unresponsive.

"Troubles Talk"

Tannen (1990b) identifies talk about troubles, or personal problems, as a kind of interaction in which hurt feelings may result from the contrast between most men's and women's rules of communication. A woman might tell her partner that she is feeling down because she did not get a job she wanted. In an effort to be supportive, he might respond by saying, "You shouldn't feel bad. Lots of people don't get jobs they want." To her this seems to dismiss her feelings—to belittle them by saying lots of people experience her situation. Yet within masculine speech communities, this is a way of showing respect for another by not assuming that she or he needs sympathy.

Now let's turn the tables and see what happens when a man feels troubled. When he meets Nancy, Craig is unusually quiet because he feels down about not getting a job offer. Sensing that something is wrong, Nancy tries to show interest by asking, "Are you okay? What's bothering you?" Craig feels she is imposing and trying to get him to show a vulnerability he prefers to keep to himself. Nancy probes further to show she cares. As a result, he feels intruded on and withdraws further. Then Nancy feels shut out.

But perhaps Craig does decide to tell Nancy why he feels down. After hearing about his rejection letter, Nancy says, "I know how you feel. I felt so low when I didn't get that position at Datanet." She is matching experiences to show Craig that she understands his feelings and that he's not alone. Within his communication rules, however, this is demeaning his situation by focusing on her, not him. When Nancy mentions her own experience, Craig thinks she is trying to steal the center stage for herself. Within his speech community, that is one way men vie for dominance and attention. Yet Nancy has learned to share similar experiences as a way to build connections with others.

The Point of the Story

Another instance in which feminine and masculine communication rules often clash and cause problems is in relating experiences. Typically, men have learned to speak in a linear manner in which they move sequentially through major points in a story to get to the climax. Their talk tends to be straightforward without a great many details. The rules of feminine speech, however, call for more

detailed and less linear storytelling. Whereas a man is likely to provide rather bare information about what happened, a woman is more likely to embed the information within a larger context of the people involved and other things going on. Women include details not because all of the specifics are important in themselves but because recounting them shows involvement and allows a conversational partner to be more fully part of the situation being described.

Because feminine and masculine rules about details differ, men often find women's way of telling stories wandering and unfocused. Conversely, men's style of storytelling may strike women as leaving out all of the interesting details. Many a discussion between women and men has ended either with his exasperated demand, "Can't you get to the point?" or with her frustrated question, "Why don't you tell me how you were feeling and what else was going on?" She wants more details than his rules call for; he is interested in fewer details than she has learned to supply.

Relationship Talk

"Can we talk about us?" is the opening of innumerable conversations that end in misunderstanding and hurt. As Tannen (1986) noted in an earlier book, *That's Not What I Meant*, men and women tend to have very different ideas about what it means to talk about relationships. In general, men are inclined to think a relationship is going fine as long as there is no need to talk about it. They are interested in discussing the relationship only if there are particular problems to be addressed. In contrast, women generally think a relationship is working well as long as they can talk about it with partners. The difference here grows out of the fact that men tend to use communication to do things and solve problems, while women generally regard the *process* of communicating as a primary way to create and sustain relationships with others. For many women, conversation is a way to be with another person—to affirm and enhance closeness. Men's different rules stipulate that communication is to achieve some goal or fix some problem. No wonder men often duck when their partners want to "discuss the relationship," and women often feel a relationship is in trouble when their partners are unwilling to talk about it.

These are only four of many situations in which feminine and masculine rules of communication may collide and cause problems. Women learn to use talk to build and sustain connections with others. Men learn that talk is to convey information and establish status. Given these distinct starting points, it's not surprising that women and men often find themselves locked into misunderstandings.

Interestingly, research (Sollie & Fischer, 1985) suggests that women and men who are androgynous are more flexible communicators, who are able to engage comfortably in both masculine and feminine styles of speech. The breadth of their communicative competence enhances the range of situations in which they can be effective in achieving various goals. On learning about different speech rules, many couples find they can improve their communication. Each partner has become bilingual, and so communication between them is smoother and more satisfying. When partners understand how to interpret each other's rules, they are less likely to misread motives. In addition, they learn how to speak the other's language, which means women and men become more gratifying conversational partners for each other, and they can enhance the quality of their relationships.

References

Aleguire, D. G. (1978). *Interruptions as turn-taking.* Paper presented at the International Sociological Association Ninth World Congress of Sociology, Uppsala University, Sweden.

Aries, E. (1987). Gender and communication. In P. Shaver & C. Hendricks (Eds.), *Sex and gender* (pp. 149–176). Newbury Park, CA: Sage.

Austin, A. M. B., Salehi, M., & Leffler, A. (1987). Gender and developmental differences in children's conversations. *Sex Roles, 16,* 497–510.

Bate, B. (1988). *Communication between the sexes.* New York: Harper and Row.

Beck, A. T. (1988). *Love is never enough.* New York: Harper and Row.

Bellinger, D. C., & Gleason, J. B. (1982). Sex differences in parental directives to young children. *Sex Roles, 8,* 1123–1139.

Campbell, K. K. (1973). The rhetoric of women's liberation: An oxymoron. *Quarterly Journal of Speech, 59,* 74–86.

Coates, J. (1986). *Women, men, and language: Studies in language and linguistics.* London: Longman.

Coates, J., & Cameron, D. (1989). *Women in their speech communities: New perspectives on language and sex.* London: Longman.

Derlega, V. J., & Chaiken, A. L. (1976). Norms affecting self-disclosure in men and women. *Journal of Consulting and Clinical Psychology, 44,* 376–380.

Eakins, B., & Eakins, G. (1976). Verbal turn-taking and exchanges in faculty dialogue. In B. L. Du Bois & I. Crouch (Eds.), *Papers in southwest English: IV. Proceedings of the conference on the sociology of the languages of American women* (pp. 53–62). San Antonio, TX: Trinity University Press.

Eakins, B. W., & Eakins, R. G. (1978). *Sex differences in human communication.* Boston, MA: Houghton Mifflin.

Fishman, P. M. (1978). Interaction: The work women do. *Social Problems, 25,* 397–406.

Hall, D., & Langellier, K. (1988). Story-telling strategies in mother-daughter communication. In B. Bate & A. Taylor (Eds.), *Women communicating: Studies of women's talk* (pp. 197–226). Norwood, NJ: Ablex.

Johnson, F. L. (1989). Women's culture and communication: An analytical perspective. In C. M. Lont & S. A. Friedley (Eds.), *Beyond Boundaries: Sex and gender diversity in communication* (pp. 301–316). Fairfax, VA: George Mason University Press.

Kemper, S. (1984). When to speak like a lady. *Sex Roles, 10,* 435–443.

Kramarae, C. (1981). *Women and men speaking: Frameworks for analysis.* Rowley, MA: Newbury House.

Labov, W. (1972). *Sociolinguistic patterns.* Philadelphia, PA: University of Pennsylvania Press.

Lakoff, R. (1975). *Language and woman's place.* New York: Harper and Row.

Langer, S. K. (1953). *Feeling and form: A theory of art.* New York: Scribner's.

Langer, S. K. (1979). *Philosophy in a new key: A study in the symbolism of reason, rite and art* (3rd ed.). Cambridge, MA: Harvard University Press.

Lewis, E. T., & McCarthy, P. R. (1988). Perceptions of self-disclosure as a function of gender-linked variables. *Sex Roles, 19,* 47–56.

Maltz, D. N., & Borker, R. (1982). A cultural approach to male-female miscommunication. In J. J. Gumpertz (Ed.), *Language and social identity* (pp. 196–216). Cambridge, UK: Cambridge University Press.

Mulac, A., Wiemann, J. M., Widenmann, S. J., & Gibson, T. W. (1988). Male/female language differences and effects in same-sex and mixed-sex dyads: The gender-linked language effect. *Communication Monographs, 55,* 315–335.

Parlee, M. B. (1979, May). Conversational politics. *Psychology Today,* pp. 48–56.

Saurer, M. K., & Eisler, R. M. (1990). The role of masculine gender roles stress in expressivity and social support network factors. *Sex Roles, 23,* 261–271.

Schaef, A. W. (1981). *Women's reality.* St. Paul, MN: Winston Press.

Sollie, D. L., & Fischer, J. L. (1985). Sex-role orientation, intimacy of topic, and target person differences in self-disclosure among women. *Sex Roles, 12,* 917–929.

Spender, D. (1984a). *Man made language.* London: Routledge and Kegan Paul.

Stewart, L. P., Stewart, A. D., Friedley, S. A., & Cooper, P. J. (1990). *Communication between the sexes: Sex differences, and sex role stereotypes* (2nd ed.). Scottsdale, AZ: Gorsuch Scarisbrick.

Tannen, D. (1986). *That's not what I meant! How conversational style makes or breaks relationships.* New York: Ballantine.

Tannen, D. (1990a). Gender differences in conversational coherence: Physical alignment and topical cohesion. In B. Dorval (Ed.), *Conversational organization and its development.* (Vol. XXXVIII, pp. 167–206). Norwood, NJ: Ablex.

Tannen, D. (1990b). *You just don't understand: Women and men in conversation.* New York: William Morrow.

Thorne, B., & Henley, N. (1975). *Language and sex: Difference and dominance.* Rowley, MA: Newbury House.

Treichler, P. A., & Kramarae, C. (1983). Women's talk in the ivory tower. *Communication Quarterly, 31,* 118–132.

West, C., & Zimmerman, D. H. (1983). Small insults: A study of interruptions in cross-sex conversations between unacquainted persons. In B. Thorne, C. Kramarae, & N. Henley (Eds.), *Language, gender and society* (pp. 102–117). Rowley, MA: Newbury House.

Wood, J. T. (1993a). Engendered relationships: Interaction, caring, power, and responsibility in close relationships. In S. Duck (Ed.), *Processes in close relationships: Contexts of close relationships* (Vol. 3). Beverly Hills, CA: Sage.

Wood, J. T. (1993b). Engendered identities: Shaping voice and mind through gender. In D. Vocate (Ed.), *Intrapersonal communication: Different voices, different minds.* Hillsdale, NJ: Lawrence Erlbaum.

Wood, J. T., & Inman, C. (1993, August). In a different mode: Recognizing male modes of closeness. *Journal of Applied Communication Research.*

Wood, J. T., & Lenze, L. F. (1991b). Gender and the development of self: Inclusive pedagogy in interpersonal communication. *Women's Studies in Communication, 14,* 1–23.

Questions for Reflection

1. Observe and reflect on your own speech patterns. To what extent is your speech style reflective of that which is typical for your gender?

2. Do the primary games you played in your childhood match those suggested by the authors for persons of your sex?

3. To what extent do your childhood socialization experiences explain your current speech style?

4. If your current speech style is not explained by your childhood experiences, to what do you attribute your style?

SELECTION FOUR

Just as the communication style of men varies from that of women because of their different experiences, so too do the styles of communication exhibited by members of other American speech communities differ from one another. Through learning about the distinctive characteristics that are valued within a particular speech community we can become better able to understand and appreciate the interactions that we have with those whose primary speech community is different from our own. In this article, Shirley N. Weber, a professor in the African-American Studies Department at San Diego State University, explains the communication and cultural functions that black language serves in the black community. Important in this analysis is the understanding that a speech community's common heritage from hundreds of years past can continue to influence its communication practices today.

The Need to Be: The Socio-Cultural Significance of Black Language

Shirley N. Weber

"Hey blood, what it is? Ah, Man, ain't notin to it but to do it."
"Huney, I done told ya', God, he don't lak ugly."
"Look-a-there. I ain't seen nothin like these economic indicators."

From the street corners to the church pew to the board room, black language is used in varying degrees. It is estimated that 80 to 90 percent of all black Americans use the black dialect as least some of the time.[1] However, despite its widespread use among blacks at all social and economic levels, there continues to be concern over its validity and continued use. Many of the concerns arise from a lack of knowledge and appreci-

ation for the history of black language and the philosophy behind its use.

Since the publication of J. L. Dillard's book *Black English* in 1972, much has been written on the subject of black language. Generally, the research focuses on the historical and linguistic validity of black English, and very little has been devoted to the communications and cultural functions black language serves in the black community. It seems obvious that given the fact that black English is not "formally" taught in schools to black children and, yet, has widespread use among blacks, it must serve some important functions in the black community that represent the black's unique experience in America. If black language served no important function, it would become extinct like other cultural relics because all languages are functional tools that change and adapt to cultural and technological demands. If

Reprinted by permission of Shirley N. Weber, Ph.D., Associate Professor, African Studies, San Diego State University.

they cease to do this, they cease to exist as living languages. (The study of the English languages' evolution and expansion over the last hundred years, to accommodate changing values and technological advancements, is a good example.) This article looks at the "need to be," the significance of black language to black people.

One's language is a model of his or her culture and of that culture's adjustment to the world. All cultures have some form of linguistic communications; without language, the community would cease to exist. To deny that a people has a language to express its unique perspective of the world is to deny its humanity. Furthermore, the study of language is a study of the people who speak that language and of the way they bring order to the chaos of the world. Consequently, the study of black language is really an examination of African people and of their adjustment to the conditions of American slavery. Smitherman says that black English (dialect) is

an Africanized form of English reflecting Black America's linguistic-cultural African heritage and the conditions of servitude, oppression and life in America. . . .

(It) is a language mixture, adapted to the conditions of slavery and discrimination, a combination of language and style interwoven with and inextricable from Afro-American culture [2]

Much has been written about the origins of black language, and even though the issue seems to be resolved for linguists, the rest of the world is still lingering under false assumptions about it. Basically, there are two opposing views: one that says there was African influence in the development of the language and the other that says there was not. Those who reject African influence believe that the African arrived in the United States and tried to speak English. And, because he lacked certain intellectual and physical attributes, he failed. This hypothesis makes no attempt to examine the phonological and grammatical structures of West African languages to see if there are any similarities. It places the African in a unique

position unlike any other immigrant to America. Linguistic rationales and analyses are given for every other group that entered America pronouncing words differently and or structuring their sentences in a unique way. Therefore, when the German said *zis* instead of *this*, America understood. But, when the African said *dis*, no one considered the fact that consonant combinations such as *th* may not exist in African languages.

Countering this dialectical hypothesis is the creole hypothesis that, as a result of contact between Africans and Europeans, a new language formed that was influenced by both languages. This language took a variety of forms, depending on whether there was French, Portuguese, or English influence. There is evidence that these languages were spoken on the west coast of Africa as early as the sixteenth century (before the slave trade). This hypothesis is further supported by studies of African languages that demonstrate the grammatical, phonological, and rhythmic similarities between them and black English. Thus, the creole hypothesis says that the African responded to the English language as do all other non-English speakers: from the phonological and grammatical constructs of the native language.

The acceptance of the creole hypothesis is the first step toward improving communications with blacks. However, to fully understand and appreciate black language and its function in the black community, it is essential to understand some general African philosophies about language and communications, and then to see how they are applied in the various styles and forms of black communications.

In Janheinz Jahn's *Muntu*, basic African philosophies are examined to give a general overview of African culture. It is important to understand that while philosophies that govern the different groups in Africa vary, some general concepts are found throughout African cultures. One of the primary principles is the belief that everything has a reason for being. Nothing simply exists without purpose or consequences. This is the basis of Jahn's explanation of the four basic elements of life, which are Muntu, mankind; Kintu, things; Hantu, place and time; and Kuntu, modality. These four elements do not exist as static objects but as forces that have consequences and influence. For instance, in Hantu, the West is not merely a place defined by geographic location, but a force that influences the East, North, and South. Thus, the term "Western world" connotes a way of life that either complements or challenges other ways of life. The Western world is seen as a force and not a place. (This is applicable to the other three elements also.)

Muntu, or man, is distinguished from the other three elements by his possession of Nommo, the magical power of the word. Without Nommo, nothing exists. Consequently, mankind, the possessor of Nommo, becomes the master of all things.

All magic is word magic, incantations and exorcism, blessings and curse. Through Nommo, the word, man establishes his mastery over things. . . .

If there were no word all forces would be frozen, there would be no procreation, no changes, no life. . . . For the word holds the course of things in train and changes and transforms them. And since the word has this power every word is an effective word, every word is binding. And the muntu is responsible for his word.[3]

Nommo is so powerful and respected in the black community that only those who are skillful users of the word become leaders. One of the main qualifications of leaders of black people is that they must be able to articulate the needs of the people in a most eloquent manner. And because Muntu is a force who controls Nommo, which has power and consequences, the speaker must generate and create movement and power within his listeners. One of the ways this is done is through the use of imaginative and vivid language. Of the five canons of speech, it is said that Inventio or invention is the most utilized in black American. Molefi Asante called it the "coming to be of the novel," or the making of the new. So that while the message might be the same, the analogies, stories, images, and so forth must be fresh, new, and alive.

Because nothing exists without Nommo, it, too, is the force that creates a sense of community among communicators, so much so that the speaker and audience become one as senders and receivers of the message. Thus, an audience listening and responding to a message is just as important as the speaker, because without their "amens" and "right-ons" the speaker may not be successful. This interplay between speaker and listeners is called "call and response" and is a part of the African world view, which holds that all elements and forces are interrelated and indistinguishable because they work together to accomplish a common goal and to create a sense of community between the speaker and the listeners.

This difference between blacks and whites was evident, recently, in a class where I lectured on Afro-American history. During the lecture, one of my more vocal black students began to respond to the message with some encouraging remarks like "all right," "make it plain," "that all right and," "teach." She was soon joined by a few more black students who gave similar comments. I noticed that this surprised and confused some of the white students. When questioned later about this, their response was that they were not used to having more than one person talk at a time, and they really could not talk and listen at the same time. They found the comments annoying and disruptive. As the lecturer, I found the comments refreshing and inspiring. The black student who initiated the responses had no difficulty understanding what I was saying while she was reacting to it, and did not consider herself "rude."

In addition to the speaker's verbal creativity and the dynamic quality of the communication environment, black speech is very rhythmic. It flows like African languages in a consonant-vowel-consonant-vowel pattern. To achieve this rhythmic effect, some syllables are held longer and are accented stronger and differently from standard English, such as DE-troit. This rhythmic pattern is learned early by young blacks and is reinforced by the various styles it complements.

With this brief background into the historical and philosophical foundation of black language, we can examine some of the styles commonly employed and their role in African-American life. Among the secular styles, the most common is *rappin'*. Although the term *rappin'* is currently used by whites to mean simply talking (as in *rap sessions*), it originally described the dialogue between a man and a woman where the main intention is to win the admiration of the woman. A man's success in rappin' depends on his ability to make creative and imaginative statements that generate interest on the part of the woman to hear more of the rap. And, although she already knows his intentions, the ritual is still played out; and, if the rap is weak, he will probably lose the woman.

To outsiders, rappin' might not appear to be an important style in the black community, but it is very important and affects the majority of black people because at some time in a black person's life, he or she will be involved in a situation where rappin' will take place. For, in the black community, it is the mating call, the introduction of the male to the female, and it is ritualistically expected by black women. So that while it is reasonable to assume that all black males will not rise to the level of "leader" in the black community because only a few will possess the unique oral skills necessary, it can be predicted that black men will have to learn how to "rap" to a woman.

Like other forms of black speech, the rap is rhythmic and has consequences. It is the good *rapper* who *gets over* (scores). And, as the master of Nommo, the rapper creates, motivates, and changes conditions through his language. It requires him to be imaginative and capable of responding to positive and negative stimuli immediately. For instance:

R: *Hey Mama, how you doing?*
L: *Fine.*
R: *Yeah, I can see! (looking her up and down) Say, you married?*
L: *Yes.*
R: *Is your husband married? (bringing humor and doubt)*

The rap requires participation by the listener. Thus, the speaker will ask for confirmation that the listener is following his line of progression. The rap is an old style that is taught to young men early. And, while each male will have his own style of rappin' that will adapt to the type of woman he is rappin' to, a poor, unimaginative rap is distasteful and often repulsive to black women.

Runnin' it down is a form of rappin' without sexual overtones. It is simply explaining something in great detail. The speaker's responsibility is to vividly recreate the event or concept for the listener so that there is complete agreement and understanding concerning the event. The speaker gives accurate descriptions of the individuals involved, describing them from head to toe. Every object and step of action is minutely described. To an outsider this might sound boring and tedious. However, it is the responsibility of the speaker to use figurative language to keep the listener's attention. In a narrative of a former slave from Tennessee, the following brief excerpt demonstrates the vivid language used in runnin' it down:

I remember Mammy told me about one master who almost starved his slaves. Mighty stingy I reckon he was.
Some of them slaves was so poorly thin they ribs would kinda rustle against each other like corn stalks a-drying in the hot winds. But they gets even one hog killing time, and it was funny, too, Mammy said.[4]

Runnin' it down is not confined to secular styles. In C. L. Franklin's sermon, "The Eagle Stirreth Her Nest"—the simple story of an eagle, mistaken for a chicken, that grows up and is eventually set free—the story becomes a drama that vividly takes the listener through each stage of the eagle's development. And even when the eagle is set free because she can no longer live in a cage, she does not simply fly away. Instead, she flies from one height to the other, surveying the surroundings, and then flies away. The details are so vivid that the listener can "see" and "feel" the events. Such is the style and the effect of runnin' it down.

Another common style of black language is *the dozens*. The dozens is a verbal battle of insults between speakers. The term dozens was used during slavery to refer to a selling technique used by slavers. If an individual had a disability, he was considered "damaged goods" and was sold with eleven other "damaged" slaves at a discount rate. The term dozens refers to negative physical characteristics. To an outsider, the dozens might appear cruel and harsh. But to members of the black community, it is the highest form of verbal warfare and impromptu speaking. The game is often played in jest.

When the dozens is played, there is usually a group of listeners that serves as judge and jury over the originality, creativity, and humor of the comments. The listeners encourage continuation of the contest by giving comments like "Ou, I wouldn't take that," "Cold," "Rough," "Stale," or any statement that assesses the quality of the comments and encourages response. The battle continues until someone wins. This is determined by the loser giving up and walking away, or losing his cool and wanting to fight. When a physical confrontation occurs, the winner is not determined by the fight, but by the verbal confrontation. The dozens is so popular that a rock 'n' roll group made a humorous recording of insults between friends. Some of the exchanges were:

Say Man, your girlfriend so ugly, she had to sneak up on a glass to get a drink of water.

Man, you so ugly, yo mamma had to put a sheet over your head so sleep could sneak up on you.

The dozens, like other forms of black language, calls on the speaker to use words to create moods. More than any other form, it pits wit against wit, and honors the skillful user of Nommo.

The final secular style to be discussed is proverbial wisdom. Sayings are used in the black community as teaching tools to impart values and truths. Their use demonstrates the African-American's respect for the oral tradition in teaching and socializing the young. Popular phrases, such as "what goes around comes around," "if you make

you bed hard you gon lay in it," "God don't like ugly," and "a hard head make a soft behind," are used in everyday conversation by blacks from all social, economic, and educational strata. At some time in a black child's life, the sayings are used to teach them what life expects of them and what they can expect in return. It is also used to expose the truth in an artful and less offensive manner, such as "you don't believe fat meat is greasy." In this saying the listener is being put down for having a narrow or inaccurate view of things. And while it might appear that proverbial wisdoms are static, they are constantly changing and new ones are being created. One of the latest is said when you believe someone is lying to you or "putting you on." It is, "pee on my head and tell me it's raining." Or, if someone is talking bad about you, you might say, "don't let your mouth write a check your ass can't cash." Proverbial wisdom can be found on every socioeconomic level in the black community, and it is transmitted from generation to generation. Listening to speech that is peppered with proverbial sayings might seem strange to nonblacks. But, because proverbial sayings are generally accepted as "truths" because they are taught to children at a very early age, they effectively sum up events and predict outcome.

Like the secular, the nonsecular realm places a tremendous emphasis on the creative abilities of the speaker. The speaker (preacher) creates experiences for his listeners, who are participants in the communication event. The minister calls and his audience responds, and at some point they become one. The minister actively seeks his audience's involvement and when he does not receive it, he chides and scolds them. The audience also believes that the delivery of a good sermon is dependent upon them encouraging the minister with their "amens" and "right-ons." And if the minister preaches false doctrine, the audience also feels obliged to tell him, "Uh, oh Reb, you done gone too far now!"

The language used by the minister, who is probably very fluent in standard English, is generally seasoned with black English. Seldom will you hear the term *Lord* used, but you will hear *Lawd* because the *Lord* is the man in the big house who is an overseer, but the *Lawd* is a friend who walks, talks, and comforts you. The relationship between the *Lawd* and his people is more personal than the *Lord's*.

Also, the speaker may overaccent a word for black emphasis. In C. L. Franklin's sermon, he said, *"extra-*ordinary sight" He then came right back and said *extraordinary*, to demonstrate that he knew how to "correctly" enunciate the word. The nonsecular style of speech is generally the most dramatic of all forms and has the highest degree of audience participation. It encompasses all the elements of black language, and of all the styles it is the most African in form.

Black language and the numerous styles that have been developed are indications of the African-American's respect for the spoken word. The language has often been called a hieroglyphic language because of the vivid picture created by the speaker for the listener about the activities or feelings taking place. To say someone is "all jawed up," or "smacking on some barnyard pimp," or "ready to hat," is more imaginative and creative than saying they had "nothing to say," or "eating chicken," or "ready to leave." The responsibility of the speaker and the listener to participate in the communication event also emphasizes the African world view, which stresses the interrelatedness of all things to each other. And finally, the dynamics of the communication, and the responsibility of man as the user of Nommo, places communication and the spoken word in the arena of forces and not static objects. The rhythm and flow of the language approximates the style and flow and unity of African life.

Despite all of the explanation of the Africanness found in black language, many continue to ask, why use it? Why do blacks who have lived in America for hundreds of years continue to speak "black"? Why do those who possess degrees of higher learning and even write scholarly articles and books in standard English continue to talk "black"?

There are many reasons for the continued use of black language. A language expresses an experience. If the experiences of a group are culturally unique, the group will need a different vocabulary to express them. If white folks in white churches don't *get happy* because they have been socialized to be quiet listeners in church, then they don't have the vocabulary that blacks have to describe levels of spiritual possession. And if they do not have curly hair, they probably do not *press* their hair or worry about *catching up* their *kitchins*. Thus, because blacks experience the world differently from other groups in America, there is a need for a language that communicates that experience.

Secondly, black language reaches across the superficial barriers of education and social position. It is the language that binds, that creates community for blacks, so that the brother in the three-piece Brooks Brothers suit can go to the local corner where folks "hang out" and say, "hey, blood, what it is?", and be one with them. Additionally, the minister's use of black language reminds the listeners of their common experiences and struggles (for example, "I been thur the storm"). Through black language, barriers that separate blacks are lowered and they are finally "home" with each other. So, for cultural identity, the code is essential to define the common elements among them.

Finally, black language usage stands as a political statement that black people are African people who have not given up a vital part of themselves in slavery: their language. They have retained the cultural link that allows them to think and to express themselves in a non-European form. As an old adage says, The namer of names is the father of things. Thus, the ability of blacks to maintain and sustain a living language shows their control over that aspect of their lives, and their determination to preserve the culture. The use of black language is the black man's defiance of white America's total indoctrination. The use of black language by choice is a reflection not of a lack of intelligence, but of a desire to retain and preserve black life styles.

The purpose of this discussion is to help others understand and appreciate black language styles and the reasons blacks speak the way they do, in hopes of building respect for cultural difference. Now the question may be asked, what does the general society do about it? Some might ask, should whites learn black English? To that question comes a resounding *no!* Black language is, first of all, not a laboratory language and it cannot be learned in a classroom. And even if you could learn definition and grammar, you would not learn the art of creative expression that is taught when you're "knee high to a duck." Thus, you would miss the elements of rhythm and style, and you would sound like invaders or foreigners.

What one should do about the language is be open-minded and not judge the speaker by European standards of expression. If you're in a classroom and the teacher is *gettin down*, don't *wig out* because the black student says "teach" Simply realize that you must become listening participants. If some *bloods* decide to use a double negative or play *the dozens*, don't assume some social theory about how they lack a father image in the home and are therefore culturally and linguistically deprived. You just might discover that they are the authors of your college English text.

The use of black language does not represent any pathology in blacks. It simply says that, as African people transplanted to America, they are a different flower whose aroma is just as sweet as other flowers. The beginning of racial understanding is the acceptance that difference is just what it is: different, not inferior. And equality does not mean sameness.

Notes

1. Geneva Smitherman. *Talkin' and Testifyin'.* (1972). Boston: Houghton Mifflin Company, p. 2.

2. Ibid., p. 3.

3. Janheinz Jahn. *Muntu.* (1961). New York: Grove Press, Inc., pp. 132–133.

4. Smitherman, *Talkin' and Tesifyin',* p. 156.

Questions for Reflection

1. Do you agree with the author that whites should not learn black English?

2. Take a piece of rap music and analyze it to see which of the elements of black English are part of it.

3. Although Weber suggests that black English is "not a laboratory language," today young non–African American people are adopting the patterns of black English. As an exercise, write a dialogue using "the dozens" form. Reflect on what made this assignment difficult or easy for you. To what extent does Weber's thesis hold true for you?

4. Take one of the speech communities to which you belong, and describe the characteristics of its distinct style. What in the culture of this community gives rise to this style?

SELECTION FIVE

This article discusses communication between ablebodied persons and persons with disabilities. Persons with disabilities view themselves as a distinct subculture. Those who are not born disabled go through an intrapersonal communication process of redefinition of self when they become disabled. Based on interviews with persons who have visible physical disabilities Dr. Dawn O. Braithwaite, a professor at Arizona State University West, discusses the communication problems that occur when members of ablebodied and disabled cultural groups interact. She concludes with several suggestions that should help ablebodied persons communicate more effectively with disabled persons.

Viewing Persons with Disabilities as a Culture

Dawn O. Braithwaite

Jonathan is an articulate, intelligent, 35-year-old man who has used a wheelchair since becoming a paraplegic when he was 20.[1] He recalls taking an ablebodied woman out to dinner at a nice restaurant. When the waitress came to take their order, she patronizingly asked his date, "And what would *he* like to eat for dinner?" At the end of the meal the waitress presented Jonathan's date with the check and thanked her for her patronage. Although it may be hard to believe the insensitivity of the waitress, this incident is not an isolated experience for persons with disabilities.

Jeff, an ablebodied student, was working with a group that included Helen, who uses a wheelchair. He recalls an incident that really embarrassed him. "I wasn't thinking and I said to the group, 'Let's run over to the student union and get some coffee.' I was mortified when I looked over at Helen and remembered that she can't walk. I

From *Intercultural Communication: A Reader*, 7th ed., eds. Larry A. Samovar and Richard E. Porter (Belmont, CA: Wadsworth, Inc., 1994), 148–154. Reprinted by permission of the author.

felt like a real jerk." Helen later described the incident with Jeff, recalling,

At yesterday's meeting, Jeff said, "Let's run over to the union" and then he looked over at me and I thought he would die. It didn't bother me and I don't know why Jeff was so embarrassed. I didn't quite know what to say. Later in the group meeting I made it a point to say, "I've got to be running along now." I hope that Jeff noticed and felt OK about what he said.

Like Jonathan's experience, this situation between Helen and Jeff is also a common experience.

There has been a growing interest in the important area of health communication among communication scholars, with a core of researchers studying communication between ablebodied persons and those with disabilities. Persons with disabilities are becoming an increasingly large and active minority in U.S. culture, with the numbers growing yearly. In some states, disabled persons constitute the largest minority group, composing as much as seven percent of the population (Wheratt, 1988). There are two reasons for the increase in the number of persons with disabilities. First, as the population ages and lives longer, more people will develop disabilities. Second, advances in medical technologies now allow persons with disabilities to survive life-threatening illnesses and injuries.

In the past, persons with disabilities were kept out of public view, but today they are mainstreaming into all facets of society. Significant legislation, like the Americans with Disabilities Act, seek to guarantee equal rights to persons with disabilities. All of us have or will have contact with persons with disabilities of some kind and many of us will find family, friends, coworkers, or even ourselves part of the disabled culture. Marie, a college student who became quadriplegic after diving into a swimming pool, says "I knew there were disabled people around, but I never thought this would happen to me. I never even knew a disabled person before I became one. If before this happened I saw a person in a wheelchair, I would have been uncomfortable and not known what to say." As persons with disabilities continue to move into the mainstream, the need for both ablebodied and disabled persons to know how to communicate with members of the other culture will continue to grow.

The purpose of this article is to discuss communication between ablebodied persons and persons with disabilities as *cultural communication* (Carbaugh, 1990). Several researchers have described the communication of disabled and ablebodied persons as cultural communication (Braithwaite, 1990; Emry & Wiseman, 1987; Padden & Humphries, 1988). That is, we must recognize that persons with disabilities develop certain unique communication characteristics that are not shared by the majority of ablebodied individuals in U.S. society. In fact, individuals who were disabled after birth must assimilate from being a member of the ablebodied majority to being a member of a minority culture (Braithwaite, 1990).

This essay presents research findings from a series of interviews with persons who have visible physical disabilities. First, we introduce the communication problems that can arise between per-

sons in the ablebodied culture and those in the disabled culture. Second, we discuss some problems with the way research into communication between ablebodied and disabled persons has been conducted. Third, we present results from the interviews. These results show persons with disabilities engaged in a process whereby they critique the prevailing stereotypes of the disabled held by the ablebodied and engage in a process that we call *redefinition*. Finally, we discuss the importance of these findings for both scholars and students of intercultural communication.

Communication Between Ablebodied and Disabled Persons

Persons with disabilities seek to overcome the barriers associated with physical disability because disability affects all areas of an individual's life: behavioral, economic, and social. When we attempt to understand the effects of disability, we must differentiate between disability and handicap. Many aspects of disability put limitations on an individual because one or more of the key life functions, such as self-care, mobility, communication, socialization, and employment, is interrupted. Disabilities are often compensated for or overcome through assisting devices, such as wheelchairs or canes, or through training. Disabilities become handicaps when the disability interacts with the physical or social environment to impede a person in some aspect of his or her life (Crewe & Athelstan, 1985). For example, a disabled individual who is paraplegic can function in the environment with wheelchairs and curb cuts, but he or she is handicapped when buildings and/or public transportation are not accessible to wheelchairs. When the society is willing and/or able to help, disabled persons have the ability to achieve increasingly independent lives (Cogswell, 1977; DeLoach & Greer, 1981).

Many physical barriers associated with disabilities can be detected and corrected, but the social barriers resulting from disabilities are much more insidious. Nowhere are the barriers more apparent than in the communication between ablebodied persons and persons with disabilities. When ablebodied and disabled persons interact, the general, stereotypical communication problem that is present in all new relationships is heightened, and both persons behave in even more constrained and less spontaneous ways, acting overly self-conscious, self-controlled, and rigid because they feel uncomfortable and uncertain (Belgrave & Mills, 1981; Weinberg, 1978). While the ablebodied person may communicate verbal acceptance to the person with the disability, his or her nonverbal behavior may communicate rejection and avoidance (Thompson, 1982). For example, the ablebodied person may speak with the disabled person but stand at a greater distance than usual, avoid eye contact, and cut the conversation short. Disability becomes a handicap, then, for persons with disabilities when they interact with ablebodied persons and experience discomfort when communicating; this feeling blocks the normal development of a relationship between them.

Most ablebodied persons readily recognize that what we have just described is representative of their own communication experiences with disabled persons. Ablebodied persons often find themselves in the situation of not knowing what is expected of them or how to act; they have been taught both to "help the handicapped" and to "treat all persons equally." For example, should we help a person with a disability open a door or should we help them up if they fall? Many ablebodied persons have offered help only to be rebuffed by the person with the disability. Ablebodied persons greatly fear saying the wrong thing, such as "See you later!" to a blind person or "Why don't you run by the store on your way home?" to a paraplegic. It is easier to avoid situations where we might have to talk with a disabled person rather than face discomfort and uncertainty.

Persons with disabilities find these situations equally uncomfortable and are well aware of the discomfort of the ablebodied person. They are able to describe both the verbal and nonverbal signals of discomfort and avoidance that ablebodied persons portray (Braithwaite, 1985, 1992). Persons with disabilities report that when they meet ablebodied persons, they want to get the discomfort "out of the way," and they want the ablebodied person to see them as a "person like anyone else," rather than focus solely on the disability (Braithwaite, 1985, 1991).

Problems with the Present Research

When we review the research in the area of communication between ablebodied and disabled persons, three problems come to the forefront. First, very little is known about the communication behavior of disabled persons. A few researchers have studied disabled persons' communication, but most of them study ablebodied persons' reactions to disabled persons (most of these researchers are themselves ablebodied). Second, most researchers talk *about* persons with disabilities, not *with* them. Disabled persons are rarely represented in the studies; when they are, the disabled person is most often "played," for example, by an ablebodied person in a wheelchair. Third, and most significantly, the research is usually conducted from the perspective of the ablebodied person; that is, what can persons with disabilities *do* to make ablebodied persons feel more comfortable It does not take into consideration the effects on the person with the disability. Therefore, we have what may be called an *ethnocentric bias* in the research, which focuses on ablebodied/disabled communication from the perspective of the ablebodied majority, ignoring the perspective of the disabled minority.

We shall discuss the results of an ongoing study that obtains the perspectives of disabled persons concerning their communication with ablebodied persons. To date, fifty-seven in-depth interviews have been conducted with physically disabled adults about their communication with ablebodied persons in the early stages of relationships. Here we are concerned with understanding human behavior from the disabled person's own frame of reference. This concern is particularly important in the area of communication between ablebodied and disabled persons and, as we have said, previous research has been conducted from the perspective of ablebodied persons; disabled persons have not participated in these studies. Doing research by talking directly to the person with the disability helps to bring out information important to the individual, rather than simply getting the disabled person's reaction to what is on the researcher's mind. This research represents a unique departure from what other researchers have been doing because the focus is on the perspective of the disabled minority.

Process of Redefinition

When discussing their communication with ablebodied persons, disabled persons' responses often deal with what we call *redefinition*. That is, in their communication with ablebodied persons and among themselves, disabled persons engage in a process whereby they critique the prevailing stereotypes held by the ablebodied and create new definitions: (1) of the disabled as members of a "new" culture; (2) of self by the disabled; (3) of disability for the disabled; and (4) of disability for the dominant culture.

Redefinition of the Disabled as Members of a "New" Culture

Persons with disabilities report seeing themselves as a minority or a culture. For some of the subjects, this definition crosses disability lines; that is, their definition of *disabled* includes all persons who have disabilities. For others, the definition is not as broad and includes only other persons with the same type of disability. Most persons with disabilities, however, do define themselves as part of a culture. Says one person:

It's (being disabled) like West Side Story. *Tony and Maria; white and Puerto Rican. They were afraid of*

each other; ignorant of each others' cultures. People are people.

According to another man:

First of all, I belong to a subculture because of the way I have to deal with things being in the medical system, welfare. There is the subculture . . . I keep one foot in the ablebodied culture and one foot in my own culture. One of the reasons I do that is so that I don't go nuts.

Membership in the disabled culture has several similarities to membership in other cultures. Many of the persons interviewed likened their own experiences to those of other cultures, particularly to African Americans and women. When comparing the disabled to both African Americans and women, we find several similarities. The oppression is biologically based, at least for those who have been disabled since birth; one is a member of the culture by being born with cerebral palsy or spina bifida, for example. As such, the condition is unalterable; the disability will be part of them throughout their lifetime.

For those persons who are not born with a disability, membership in the culture can be a process that emerges over time. For some, the process is a slow one, as in the case of a person with a degenerative disease that may develop over many years and gradually become more and more severe. If a person has a sudden-onset disability, such as breaking one's neck in an accident and waking up a quadraplegic, the movement from a member of the dominant culture— "normal person"—to the minority culture—disabled person—may happen in a matter of seconds. This sudden transition to membership in the disabled culture presents many challenges of readjustment in all facets of an individual's life, especially in communication relationships with others.

Redefinition of Self by the Disabled

How one redefines oneself, then, from normal or ablebodied to disabled, is a process of redefinition of self. While African Americans struggle for identity in a white society and women struggle for identity in a male-dominated society, the disabled struggle for identity in an ablebodied world. One recurring theme from the participants in this study is "I am a person like anyone else" (if disabled since birth) or "I'm basically the same person I always was" (if a sudden-onset disability). The person who is born with a disability learns the process of becoming identified as "fully human" while still living as a person with a disability. The individual who is disabled later in life, Goffman (1963) contends, goes through a process of redefinition of self. For example, the subjects born with disabilities make such statements as "I am not different from anyone else as far as I am concerned" or "Disability does not mean an incomplete character." Persons whose disabilities happened later say "You're the same person you were. You just don't do the same things you did before." One man put it this way:

If anyone refers to me as an amputee, that is guaranteed to get me madder than hell! I don't deny the leg amputation, but I am me. I am a whole person. One.

During the redefinition process, individuals come to terms with both positive and negative ramifications of disability. Some subjects report that "disability is like slavery to me." In contrast, one woman reports:

I find myself telling people that this has been the worst thing that has happened to me. It has also been one of the best things. It forced me to examine what I felt about myself . . . confidence is grounded in me, not in other people. As a woman, not as dependent on clothes, measurements, but what's inside me.

One man expresses his newfound relationship to other people when he says, "I'm more interdependent than I was. I'm much more aware of that now." This process of redefinition is evident in what those interviewed have to say.

Redefinition of Disability for the Disabled

A third category of redefinition occurs as persons with disabilities redefine both disability and its associated characteristics. For example, in redefining disability itself, one man said, "People will say, 'Thank God I'm not handicapped.' And I'll say, 'Let's see, how tall are you? Tell me how you get something off that shelf up there!'" This perspective is centered on the view of the disability as a characteristic of the person rather than the person himself; it recognizes disability as situational rather than inherent or grounded in the person. In this view, everyone is disabled to some extent: by race, gender, height, or physical abilities, for example.

Redefinition of disability can be seen in the use of language. Says one subject who objected to the label *handicapped person*: "Persons with a handicapping condition. You emphasize that person's identity and then you do something about the condition." This statement ties into viewing one's self as a person first. Research reveals movement from the term *handicapped* to *disability* or *disabled*, although a wide variety of terms are used by these subjects to talk about the self. Another change in language has been the avoidance of phrases such as "polio victim" or "arthritis sufferer." Again the emphasis is on the person, not the disability. "I am a person whose arms and legs do not function very well," says one subject who had polio as a child.

There have also been changes in the terms that refer to ablebodied persons. Says one man:

You talk about the ablebodied. I will talk about the nonhandicapped . . . Its a different kind of mode. In Michigan they've got it in the law: "temporarily ablebodied."

It is common for the persons interviewed to refer to the majority in terms of the minority: "nondisabled" or "nonhandicapped," rather than "ablebodied" or "normal" More than the change in terminology, the phrase "temporarily ablebodied" or TABS serves to remind ablebodied persons that no one is immune from disability. The persons interviewed also used TABS as a humorous reference term for the ablebodied as well. "Everyone is a TAB." This view jokingly intimates, "I just got mine earlier than you . . . just you wait!"

In addition to redefining disability, the disabled also redefine "assisting devices":

Now, there were two girls about eight playing and I was in my shorts. And I'll play games with them and say, "which is my good leg?" And that gets them to thinking. Well, this one (pats artificial leg) is not nearly as old as the other one!

Says another subject:

Do you know what a cane is? It's a portable railing! The essence of a wheelchair is a seat and wheels. Now, I don't know that a tricycle is not doing the exact same thing.

Again, in these examples, the problem is not the disability or the assisting device, such as a cane, but how one views the disability or the assisting device. These assisting devices take on a different meaning for the persons using them. Subjects expressed frustration with persons who played with their wheelchairs: "This chair is not a toy, it is part of me. When you touch my chair, you are touching me." One woman, a business executive, expanded on this by saying, "I don't know why people who push my chair feel compelled to make car sounds as they do it."

Redefinition of Disability for the Dominant Culture

Along with the redefinitions that concern culture, self, and disability comes an effort to try to change society's view of the disabled and disability (Braithwaite, 1990). Persons with disabilities are attempting to change the view of themselves as helpless, as victims, or merely sick. One man says:

People do not consider you, they consider the chair first. I was in a store with my purchases on my lap and money on my lap. The clerk looked at my companion and said, "Cash or charge?"

This incident with the clerk is a story that has been voiced by every person interviewed in some form or another, just as it happened to Jonathan at the restaurant with his date. One woman who has multiple sclerosis and uses a wheelchair told of her husband accompanying her while she was shopping for lingerie. When they were in front of the lingerie counter, she asked for what she wanted, and the clerk repeatedly talked only to her husband saying, "And what size does she want?" The woman told her the size and the clerk looked at the husband and said, "and what color?" Persons with disabilities recognize that ablebodied persons often see them as disabled first and persons second (if at all), and they express a need to change this view. Says a man who has muscular dystrophy:

I do not believe in those goddamned telethons . . . they're horrible, absolutely horrible. They get into the self-pity, you know, and disabled folk do not need that. Hit people in terms of their attitudes and then try to deal with and process their feelings. And the telethons just go for the heart and leave it there.

Most of the subjects indicate they see themselves as educators or ambassadors for all persons with disabilities. All indicate they will answer questions put to them about their disabilities, as long as they determine the other "really wants to know, to learn." One man suggests a solution:

What I am concerned with is anything that can do away with the "us" versus "them" distinction. Well, you and I are anatomically different, but we're two human beings! And at the point we can sit down and communicate eyeball to eyeball . . . the quicker you do that, the better!

Individually and collectively, persons with disabilities do identify themselves as part of a culture. They are involved in a process of redefinition of disability, both for themselves and for the ablebodied.

Conclusions

This research justifies the usefulness of viewing disability from an intercultural perspective. Persons with disabilities do see themselves as members of a culture, and viewing communication between ablebodied and disabled persons from this perspective sheds new light on the communication problems that exist. Emry and Wiseman (1987) argue that intercultural training should be the focus in our perceptions of self and others: They call for unfreezing old attitudes about disability and refreezing new ones. Clearly, from these findings, that is exactly what persons with disabilities are doing, both for themselves and for others.

Of the fifty-seven persons with disabilities interviewed, only a small percentage had any sort of education or training concerning communication, during or after rehabilitation, that would prepare them for changes in their communication relationships due to their disabilities. Such education seems especially critical for those who experience sudden onset disabilities because their self-concepts and all of their relationships undergo sudden, radical changes. Intercultural communication scholars have the relevant background and experience for this kind of research and training, and they can help make this transition from majority to minority an easier one (Emry & Wiseman, 1987; Smith, 1989).

As for ablebodied persons who communicate with disabled persons, this intercultural perspective leads to the following suggestions:

Don't assume that persons with disabilities cannot speak for themselves or do things for themselves.

Do assume they can do something unless they communicate otherwise.

Don't force your help on persons with disabilities.

Do let them tell you if they want something, what they want, and when they want it. If a person with a disability refuses your help, don't go ahead and help anyway.

Don't avoid communication with persons who have disabilities simply because you are uncomfortable or unsure.

Do remember that they have experienced others' discomfort before and understand how you might be feeling.

Do treat persons with disabilities as *persons first,* recognizing that you are not dealing with a disabled person but with a *person* who has a disability.

Note

1. The names of all the participants in these studies have been changed to protect their privacy.

References

Belgrave, F. Z., and Mills, J. (1981). "Effect upon Desire for Social Interaction with a Physically Disabled Person of Mentioning the Disability in Different Contexts." *Journal of Applied Social Psychology,* 11(1), 44-57.

Braithwaite, D. O. (February, 1985). "Impression Management and Redefinition of Self by Persons with Disabilities." Paper presented at the annual meeting of the Speech Communication Association, Denver, Colorado.

Braithwaite, D. O. (1990). "From Majority to Minority: An Analysis of Cultural Change from Ablebodied to Disabled." *International Journal of Intercultural Relations,* 14, 465-483.

Braithwaite, D. O. (1991). "Just How Much Did that Wheelchair Cost?: Management of Privacy Boundaries by Persons with Disabilities." *Western Journal of Speech Communication,* 55, 254-274.

Braithwaite, D. O. (1992). "Isn't It Great that People Like You Get Out: Communication Between Disabled and Ablebodied Persons." In E. B. Ray (Ed.) *Case Studies in Health Communication.* Lawrence Erlbaum Associates, Publishers.

Carbaugh, D. (Ed.). 1990. *Cultural Communication and Intercultural Contact.* Hillsdale, NJ: Lawrence Erlbaum Associates, Publishers.

Cogswell, Betty E. (1977). "Self Socialization: Readjustments of Paraplegics in the Community." In R. P. Marinelli and A. E. Dell Orto (Eds.), *The Psychological and Social Impact of Physical Disability,* pp. 151-159. New York: Springer Publishing Company.

Crewe, N., and Athelstan, G. (1985). *Social and Psychological Aspects of Physical Disability.* Minneapolis: University of Minnesota, Department of Independent Study and University Resources.

DeLoach, C., and Greer, B. G. (1981). *Adjustment to Severe Disability.* New York: McGraw-Hill Book Company.

Emry, R., and Wiseman, R. L. (1987). "An Intercultural Understanding of Ablebodied and Disabled Persons' Communication." *International Journal of Intercultural Relations*, 11, 7-27.

Goffman, E. (1963). *Stigma: Notes on the Management of Spoiled Identity.* New York: Simon & Schuster.

Padden, C., and Humphries, T (1988). *Deaf in America: Voices from a Culture.* Cambridge, MA: Harvard University Press.

Smith, D. H. (1989). "Studying Health Communication: An Agenda for the Future." *Health Communication*, 1(1), 17-27.

Thompson, T L. (1982). "Disclosure as a Disability-Management Strategy: A Review and Conclusions." *Communication Quarterly*, 30, 196-202.

Weinberg, N. (1978). "Modifying Social Stereotypes of the Physically Disabled." *Rehabilitation Counselling Bulletin*, 22(2), 114-124.

Wheratt, R. (August 1,1988). "Minnesota Disabled to Be Heard." *Star Tribune*, 1, 6.

Questions for Reflection

1. How do you feel when you encounter someone with a disability? Why do you suppose that you have these feelings?

2. Dr. Braithwaite concludes her article with suggestions for ablebodied persons who communicate with persons with disabilities. What suggestions can you think of for persons with disabilities who communicate with ablebodied persons?

SELECTION SIX

In your textbook you read about how nonverbal communication behaviors influence the interactions that occur and the meanings that are shared among people. The way that a person behaves with respect to time is one of these nonverbal elements. Many negative stereotypes and instances of hard feelings occur because of the common misconception that everyone views time in the same way. In this article excerpted from his book *The Dance of Life: The Other Dimension of Time*, Edward T. Hall suggests that there are at least two distinct systems for viewing time. Each of these systems is explained and its strengths and weaknesses are discussed. By understanding each system, we can become better able to accept and adapt to the time system used by those with whom we interact. This understanding should permit us to interpret others' temporal behaviors more correctly as well as enable us to adapt our own behavior in order to be contextually appropriate.

Monochronic and Polychronic Time

Edward T. Hall

Lorenzo Hubbell, trader to the Navajo and the Hopi, was three quarters Spanish and one quarter New Englander, but culturally he was Spanish to the core. Seeing him for the first time on government business transactions relating to my work in the 1930s, I felt embarrassed and a little shy because he didn't have a regular office where people could talk in private. Instead, there was a large corner room—part of his house adjoining the trading post—in which business took place. Business covered everything from visits with officials and friends, conferences with Indians who had come to see him, who also most often needed to borrow money or make sheep

deals, as well as a hundred or more routine transactions with store clerks and Indians who had not come to see Lorenzo specifically but only to trade. There were long-distance telephone calls to his warehouse in Winslow, Arizona, with cattle buyers, and his brother, Roman, at Ganado, Arizona—all this and more (some of it quite personal), carried on in public, in front of our small world for all to see and hear. If you wanted to learn about the life of an Indian trader or the ins and outs of running a small trading empire (Lorenzo had a dozen posts scattered throughout northern Arizona), all you had to do was to sit in Lorenzo's office for a month or so and take note of what was going on. Eventually all the different parts of the pattern would unfold before your eyes, as eventually they did before mine, as I lived and worked on that reservation over a five-year period.

From *The Dance of Life: The Other Dimension of Time* by Edward T. Hall, © 1983. Used by permission of Doubleday, a division of Bantam, Doubleday, Dell Publishing Group, Inc.

I was prepared for the fact that the Indians do things differently from AE cultures because I had spent part of my childhood on the Upper Rio Grande River with the Pueblo Indians as friends. Such differences were taken for granted. But this public, everything-at-once, mélange way of conducting business made an impression on me. There was no escaping it, here was another world, but in this instance, although both Spanish and Anglos had their roots firmly planted in European soil, each handled time in radically different ways.

It didn't take long for me to accustom myself to Lorenzo's business ambiance. There was so much going on that I could hardly tear myself away. My own work schedule won out, of course, but I did find that the Hubbell store had a pull like a strong magnet, and I never missed an opportunity to visit with Lorenzo. After driving through Oraibi, I would pull up next to his store, park my pickup, and go through the side door to the office. These visits were absolutely necessary because without news of what was going on life could become precarious. Lorenzo's desert "salon" was better than a newspaper, which, incidentally, we lacked.

Having been initiated to Lorenzo's way of doing business, I later began to notice similar mutual involvement in events among the New Mexico Spanish. I also observed the same patterns in Latin America, as well as in the Arab world. Watching my countrymen's reactions to this "many things at a time" system I noted how deeply it affected the channeling and flow of information, the shape and form of the networks connecting people, and a host of other important social and cultural features of the society. I realized that there was more to this culture pattern than one might at first suppose.

Years of exposure to other cultures demonstrated that complex societies organize time in at least two different ways: events scheduled as separate items—one thing at a time—as in North Europe, or following the Mediterranean model of involvement in several things at once. The two systems are logically and empirically quite distinct. Like oil and water, they don't mix. Each has its strengths as well as its weaknesses. I have termed doing many things at once: Polychronic, P-time. The North European system—doing one thing at a time—is Monochronic, M-time. P-time stresses involvement of people and completion of transactions rather than adherence to preset schedules. Appointments are not taken as seriously and, as a consequence, are frequently broken. P-time is treated as less tangible than M-time. For polychronic people, time is seldom experienced as "wasted," and is apt to be considered a point rather than a ribbon or a road, but that point is often sacred. An Arab will say, "I will see you before one hour," or "I will see you after two days." What he means in the first instance is that it will not be longer than an hour before he sees you, and at least two days in the second instance. These commitments are taken quite seriously as long as one remains in the P-time pattern.

Once, in the early '60s, when I was in Patras, Greece, which is in the middle of the P-time belt, my own time system was thrown in my face under rather ridiculous but still amusing circumstances. An impatient Greek hotel clerk, anxious to get me and my menage settled in some quarters which were far from first-class, was pushing me to make a commitment so he could continue with his siesta. I couldn't decide whether to accept this rather forlorn "bird in the hand" or take a chance on another hotel that looked, if possible, even less inviting. Out of the blue, the clerk blurted, "Make up your mind. After all, time is money!" How would you reply to that at a time of day when literally nothing was happening? I couldn't help but laugh at the incongruity of it all. If there ever was a case of time not being money, it was in Patras during siesta in the summer.

Though M-time cultures tend to make a fetish out of management, there are points at which M-time doesn't make as much sense as it might. Life in general is at times unpredictable; and who can tell exactly how long a particular client, patient, or set of transactions will take. These are imponderables in the chemistry of human transactions.

What can be accomplished one day in ten minutes, may take twenty minutes on the next. Some days people will be rushed and can't finish; on others, there is time to spare, so they "waste" the remaining time.

In Latin America and the Middle East, North Americans can frequently be psychologically stressed. Immersed in a polychronic environment in the markets, stores, and souks of Mediterranean and Arab countries, one is surrounded by other customers all vying for the attention of a single clerk who is trying to wait on everyone at once. There is no recognized order as to who is to be served next, no queue or numbers to indicate who has been waiting the longest. To the North European or American, it appears that confusion and clamor abound. In a different context, the same patterns can be seen operating in the governmental bureaucracies of Mediterranean countries: a typical office layout for important officials frequently includes a large reception area (an ornate version of Lorenzo Hubbell's office), outside the private suite, where small groups of people can wait and be visited by the minister or his aides. These functionaries do most of their business outside in this semipublic setting, moving from group to group conferring with each in turn. The semi-private transactions take less time, give others the feeling that they are in the presence of the minister as well as other important people with whom they may also want to confer. Once one is used to this pattern, it is clear that there are advantages which frequently outweigh the disadvantages of a series of private meetings in the inner office.

Particularly distressing to Americans is the way in which appointments are handled by polychronic people. Being on time simply doesn't mean the same thing as it does in the United States. Matters in a polychronic culture seem in a constant state of flux. Nothing is solid or firm, particularly plans for the future; even important plans may be changed right up to the minute of execution.

In contrast, people in the Western world find little in life exempt from the iron hand of M-time.

Time is so thoroughly woven into the fabric of existence that we are hardly aware of the degree to which it determines and coordinates everything we do, including the molding of relations with others in many subtle ways. In fact, social and business life, even one's sex life, is commonly schedule-dominated. By scheduling, we compartmentalize; this makes it possible to concentrate on one thing at a time, but it also reduces the context. Since scheduling by its very nature selects what will and will not be perceived and attended, and permits only a limited number of events within a given period, what gets scheduled constitutes a system for setting priorities for both people and functions. Important things are taken up first and allotted the most time; unimportant things are left to last or omitted if time runs out.

M-time is also tangible; we speak of it as being saved, spent, wasted, lost, made up, crawling, killed, and running out. These metaphors must be taken seriously. M-time scheduling is used as a classification system that orders life. The rules apply to everything except birth and death. It should be mentioned, that without schedules or something similar to the M-time system, it is doubtful that our industrial civilization could have developed as it has. There are other consequences. Monochronic time seals off one or two people from the group and intensifies relationships with one other person or, at most, two or three people. M-time in this sense is like a room with a closed door ensuring privacy. The only problem is that you must vacate the "room" at the end of the allotted fifteen minutes or an hour, a day, or a week, depending on the schedule, and make way for the next person in line. Failure to make way by intruding on the time of the next person is not only a sign of extreme egocentrism and narcissism, but just plain bad manners.

Monochronic time is arbitrary and imposed, that is, learned. Because it is so thoroughly learned and so thoroughly integrated into our culture, it is treated as though it were the only natural and logical way of organizing life. Yet, it is *not* inherent in man's biological rhythms or his creative drives, nor is it existential in nature.

Schedules can and frequently do cut things short just when they are beginning to go well. For example, research funds run out just as the results are beginning to be achieved. How often has the reader had the experience of realizing that he is pleasurably immersed in some creative activity, totally unaware of time, solely conscious of the job at hand, only to be brought back to "reality" with the rude shock of realizing that other, frequently inconsequential previous commitments are bearing down on him?

Some Americans associate schedules with reality, but M-time can alienate us from ourselves and from others by reducing context. It subtly influences how we think and perceive the world in segmented compartments. This is convenient in linear operations but disastrous in its effect on nonlinear creative tasks. Latino peoples are an example of the opposite. In Latin America, the intelligentsia and the academicians frequently participate in several fields at once—fields which the average North American academician, business, or professional person thinks of as antithetical. Business, philosophy, medicine, and poetry, for example, are common, well-respected combinations.

Polychronic people such as the Arabs and Turks, who are almost never alone, even in the home, make very different uses of "screening" than Europeans do. They interact with several people at once and are continually involved with each other. Tight scheduling is therefore difficult, if not impossible.

Theoretically, when considering social organization, P-time systems should demand a much greater centralization of control and be characterized by a rather shallow or simple structure. This is because the leader deals continually with many people, most of whom stay informed as to what is happening. The Arab fellah can always see his sheik. There are no intermediaries between man and sheik or between man and God. The flow of information as well as people's need to stay in-

formed complement each other. Polychronic people are so deeply immersed in each other's business that they feel a compulsion to keep in touch. Any stray scrap of a story is gathered in and stored away. Their knowledge of each other is truly extraordinary. Their involvement in people is the very core of their existence. This has bureaucratic implications. For example, delegation of authority and a buildup in bureaucratic levels are not required to handle high volumes of business. The principal shortcoming of P-type bureaucracies is that as functions increase, there is a proliferation of small bureaucracies that really are not set up to handle the problems of outsiders. In fact, outsiders traveling or residing in Latin American or Mediterranean countries find the bureaucracies unusually cumbersome and unresponsive. In polychronic countries, one has to be an insider or have a "friend" who can make things happen. All bureaucracies are oriented inward, but P-type bureaucracies are especially so.

There are also interesting points to be made concerning the act of administration as it is conceived in these two settings. Administration and control of polychronic peoples in the Middle East and Latin America is a matter of job analysis. Administration consists of taking each subordinate's job and identifying the activities that go to make up the job. These are then labeled and frequently indicated on the elaborate charts with checks to make it possible for the administrator to be sure that each function has been performed. In this way, it is felt that absolute control is maintained over the individual. Yet, scheduling how and when each activity is actually performed is left up to the employee. For an employer to schedule a subordinate's work for him would be considered a tyrannical violation of his individuality—an invasion of the self.

In contrast, M-time people schedule the activity and leave the analysis of the activities of the job to the individual. A P-type analysis, even though technical by its very nature, keeps reminding the subordinate that his job is not only a system but also part of a larger system. M-type people, on the other hand, by virtue of compartmentalization, are less likely to see their activities in context as part of the larger whole. This does not mean that they are unaware of the "organization"—far from it—only that the job itself or even the goals of the organization are seldom seen as a whole.

Giving the organization a higher priority than the functions it performs is common in our culture. This is epitomized in television, where we allow the TV commercials, the "special message," to break the continuity of even the most important communication. There is a message all right, and the message is that art gives way to commerce—polychronic advertising agencies impose their values on a monochronic population. In monochronic North European countries, where patterns are more homogeneous, commercial interruptions of this sort are not tolerated. There is a strict limit as to the number as well as the times when commercials can be shown. The average American TV program has been allotted one or two hours, for which people have set aside time, and is conceived, written, directed, acted, and played as a unity. Interjecting commercials throughout the body of the program breaks that continuity and flies in the face of one of the core systems of the culture. The polychronic Spanish treat the main feature as a close friend or relative who should not be disturbed and let the commercials mill around in the antechamber outside. My point is not that one system is superior to another, it's just that the two don't mix. The effect is disruptive, and reminiscent of what the English are going through today, now that the old monochronic queuing patterns have broken down as a consequence of a large infusion of polychronic peoples from the colonies.

Both M-time and P-time systems have strengths as well as weaknesses. There is a limit to the speed with which jobs can be analyzed, although once analyzed, proper reporting can enable a P-time administrator to handle a surprising number of subordinates. Nevertheless, organizations run on the polychronic model are limited in size, they depend on having gifted people at the top, and are slow and cumbersome when dealing with anything that is new or different. Without gifted people, a P-type bureaucracy can be a disaster. M-type organizations go in the opposite direction. They can and do grow much larger than the P-type. However, they combine bureaucracies instead of proliferating them, e.g., with consolidated schools, the business conglomerate, and the new superdepartments we are developing in government.

The blindness of the monochronic organization is to the humanity of its members. The weakness of the polychronic type lies in its extreme dependence on the leader to handle contingencies and stay on top of things. M-type bureaucracies, as they grow larger, turn inward; oblivious to their own structure, they grow rigid and are apt to lose sight of their original purpose. Prime examples are the Army Corps of Engineers and the Bureau of Reclamation, which wreak havoc on our environment in their dedicated efforts to stay in business by building dams or aiding the flow of rivers to the sea.

At the beginning of this chapter, I stated that "American time is monochronic." On the surface, this is true, but in a deeper sense, American (AE) time is both polychronic and monochronic. M-time dominates the official worlds of business, government, the professions, entertainment, and sports. However, in the home—particularly the more traditional home in which women are the core around which everything revolves—one finds that P-time takes over. How else can one raise several children at once, run a household, hold a job, be a wife, mother, nurse, tutor, chauffeur, and general fixer-upper? Nevertheless, most of us automatically equate P-time with informal activities and with the multiple tasks and responsibilities and ties of women to networks of people. At the preconscious level, M-time is male time and P-time is female time, and the ramifications of this difference are considerable.

In the conclusion of an important book, *Unfinished Business*, Maggie Scarf vividly illustrates this point. Scarf addresses herself to the question of why it is that depression (the hidden illness of our age) is three to six times more prevalent in women than it is in men. How does time equate with depression in women? It so happens that the time system of the dominant culture adds another source of trauma and alienation to the already overburdened psyches of many American women. According to Scarf, depression comes about in part as a consequence of breaking significant ties that make up most women's worlds. In our culture, men as a group tend to be more task-oriented, while women's lives center on networks of people and their relations with people. Traditionally, a woman's world is a world of human emotions, of love, attachment, envy, anxiety, and hate. This is a little difficult for late-twentieth-century people to accept because it implies basic differences between men and women that are not fashionable at the moment. Nevertheless, for most cultures around the world, the feminine mystique is intimately identified with the development of the human relations side of the personality rather than the technical, cortical left-brain occupational side. In the United States, AE women live in a world of peoples and relationships and their egos become spread out among those who are closest to them by a process we call identification. When the relationships are threatened or broken or something happens to those to whom one is close, there are worries and anxieties, and depression is a natural result.

Polychronic cultures are by their very nature oriented to people. Any human being who is naturally drawn to other human beings and who lives in a world dominated by human relationships will be either pushed or pulled toward the polychronic end of the time spectrum. If you value people, you must hear them out and cannot cut them off simply because of a schedule.

M-time, on the other hand, is oriented to tasks, schedules, and procedures. As anyone who has had experience with our bureaucracies knows, schedules and procedures take on a life all their own without reference to either logic or human needs. And it is this set of written and unwritten

rules—and the consequences of these rules—that is at least partially responsible for the reputation of American business being cut off from human beings and unwilling to recognize the importance of employee morale. Morale may well be the deciding factor in whether a given company makes a profit or not. Admittedly, American management is slowly, very slowly, getting the message. The problem is that modern management has accentuated the monochronic side at the expense of the less manageable, and less predictable, polychronic side. Virtually everything in our culture works for and rewards a monochronic view of the world. But the antihuman aspect of M-time is alienating, especially to women. Unfortunately, too many women have "bought" the M-time world, not realizing that unconscious sexism is part of it. The pattern of an entire system of time is too large, too diffuse, and too ubiquitous for most to identify its patterns. Women sense there is something alien about the way in which modern organizations handle time, beginning with how the workday, the week, and the year are set up. Such changes as flextime do not alter the fact that as soon as one enters the door of the office, one becomes immediately locked into a monochronic, monolithic structure that is virtually impossible to change.

There are other sources of tension between people who have internalized these two systems. Keep in mind that polychronic individuals are oriented toward people, human relationships, and the family, which is the core of their existence. Family takes precedence over everything else. Close friends come next. In the absence of schedules, when there is a crisis the family always comes first. If a monochronic woman has a polychronic hairdresser, there will inevitably be problems, even if she has a regular appointment and is scheduled at the same time each week. In circumstances like these, the hairdresser (following his or her own pattern) will inevitably feel compelled to "squeeze people in." As a consequence, the regular customer, who has scheduled her time very carefully (which is why she has a standing appointment in the first place), is kept waiting and feels put down, angry, and frustrated. The hairdresser is also in a bind because if he does not accommodate his relative or friend regardless of the schedule, the result is endless repercussions within his family circle. Not only must he give preferential treatment to relatives, but the degree of accommodation and who is pushed aside or what is pushed aside is itself a communication!

The more important the customer or business that is disrupted, the more reassured the hairdresser's polychronic Aunt Nell will feel. The way to ensure the message that one is accepted or loved is to call up at the last minute and expect everyone to rearrange everything. If they don't, it can be taken as a clear signal that they don't care enough. The M-time individual caught in this P-time pattern has the feeling either that he is being pressured or that he simply doesn't count. There are many instances where culture patterns are on a collision course and there can be no resolution until the point of conflict is identified. One side or the other literally gives up. In the instance cited above, it is the hairdresser who usually loses a good customer. Patterns of this variety are what maintain ethnicity. Neither pattern is right, only different, and it is important to remember that they do not mix.

Not all M-times and P-times are the same. There are tight and loose versions of each. The Japanese, for example, in the official business side of their lives where people do not meet on a highly personalized basis, provide us an excellent example of tight M-time. When an American professor, business person, technical expert, or consultant visits Japan, he may find that his time is like a carefully packed trunk—so tightly packed, in fact, that it is impossible to squeeze one more thing into the container. On a recent trip to Japan, I was contacted by a well-known colleague who had translated one of my earlier books. He wanted to see me and asked if he could pick me up at my hotel at twelve-fifteen so we could have lunch together. I had situated myself in the lobby a few minutes early, as the Japanese are almost always

prompt. At twelve-seventeen, I could see his tense figure darting through the crowd of arriving business people and politicians who had collected near the door. Following greetings, he ushered me outside to the ubiquitous black limousine with chauffeur, with white doilies covering the arms and headrests. The door of the car had hardly closed when he started outlining our schedule for the lunch period by saying that he had an appointment at three o'clock to do a TV broadcast. That set the time limit and established the basic parameters in which everyone knew where he would be at any given part of the agenda. He stated these limits—a little over two hours—taking travel time into account.

My colleague next explained that not only were we to have lunch, but he wanted to tape an interview for a magazine. That meant lunch and an interview which would last thirty to forty minutes. What else? Ah, yes. He hoped I wouldn't mind spending time with Mr. X, who had published one of my earlier books in Japanese, because Mr. X was very anxious to pin down a commitment on my part to allow him to publish my next book. He was particularly eager to see me because he missed out on publishing the last two books, even though he had written me in the United States. Yes, I did remember that he had written, but his letter arrived after the decision on the Japanese publisher had been made by my agent. That, incidentally, was the very reason why he wanted to see me personally. Three down and how many more to go? Oh, yes, there would be some photographers there and he hoped I wouldn't mind if pictures were taken? The pictures were to be both formal group shots. which were posed, and informal, candid shots during the interview, as well as pictures taken with Mr. X. As it turned out, there were at least two sets of photographers as well as a sound man, and while it wasn't "60 Minutes," there was quite a lot of confusion (the two sets of photographers each required precious seconds to straighten things out) I had to hand it to everyone—they were not only extraordinarily skilled and well organized, but also polite and considerate. Then, he hoped I wouldn't mind but there was a young man who was studying communication who had scored over 600 on an examination, which I was told put him 200 points above the average. This young man would be joining us for lunch. I didn't see how we were going to eat anything, much less discuss issues of mutual interest. In situations such as these, one soon learns to sit back, relax, and let the individual in charge orchestrate everything. The lunch was excellent, as I knew it would be—hardly leisurely, but still very good.

All the interviews and the conversation with the student went off as scheduled. The difficulties came when I had to explain to the Japanese publisher that I had no control over my own book—that once I had written a book and handed it in to my publisher, the book was marketed by either my publisher or my agent. Simply being first in line did not guarantee anything. I had to try to make it clear that I was tied into an already existing set of relationships with attached obligations and that there were other people who made these decisions. This required some explaining, and I then spent considerable time trying to work out a method for the publisher to get a hearing with my agent. This is sometimes virtually impossible because each publisher and each agent in the United States has its own representative in Japan. Thus an author is in their hands, too.

We did finish on time—pretty much to everyone's satisfaction, I believe. My friend departed on schedule as the cameramen were putting away their equipment and the sound man was rolling up his wires and disconnecting his microphones. The student drove me back to my hotel on schedule, a little after 3 P.M.

The pattern is not too different from schedules for authors in the United States. The difference is that in Japan the tightly scheduled monochronic pattern is applied to foreigners who are not well enough integrated into the Japanese system to be able to do things in a more leisurely manner, and where emphasis is on developing a good working relationship.

All cultures with high technologies seem to incorporate both polychronic as well as monochronic functions. The point is that each does it in its own way. The Japanese are polychronic when looking and working inward, toward themselves. When dealing with the outside world, they have adopted the dominant time system which characterizes that world. That is, they shift to the monochronic mode and, characteristically, since these are technical matters, they outshine us. . . .

Questions for Reflection

1. Are you a P-time or an M-time person? Give examples that prove your point.

2. How did you come to use time as you do?

3. Has this article changed your view of other people and their use of time?

4. How can M-time and P-time people avoid or resolve the differences that they are likely to experience when they set a time to meet?

SELECTION SEVEN

Interpersonal communication often occurs within a group or organizational context. Your text discusses the special processes associated with group communication. Among these is the way in which member acceptance and compliance with group norms leads to cohesion. Generally we think of a cohesive group as desirable. In this article Patricia Yancey Martin, a professor of Sociology at Florida State University, and Robert A. Hummer, a graduate student, report the results of a case study in which the norms that developed and the cohesion that resulted were unacceptable to civilized society. The value of this article is twofold. First, it should alert you to the powerful effect group dynamics can have on individual behavior. And second, it should re-emphasize the role that communication and interaction play in shaping how we view and subsequently treat other persons.

Fraternities and Rape on Campus

Patricia Yancey Martin and Robert A. Hummer

Rapes are perpetrated on dates, at parties, in chance encounters, and in specially planned circumstances. That group structure and processes, rather than individual values or characteristics, are the impetus for many rape episodes was documented by Blanchard (1959) 30 years ago (also see Geis 1971), yet sociologists have failed to pursue this theme (for an exception, see Chancer 1987). A recent review of research (Muehlenhard and Linton 1987) on sexual violence, or rape, devotes only a few pages to the situational context of rape events, and these are conceptualized as potential risk factors for individuals rather than qualities of rape-prone social contexts.

Many rapes, far more than come to the public's attention, occur in fraternity houses on college

From *Gender & Society*, Vol. 3, No. 4, December 1989, 457–473. © 1989 Sociologists for Women in Society. Reprinted by permission of Sage Publications, Inc.

and university campuses, yet little research has analyzed fraternities at American colleges and universities as rape-prone contexts (cf. Ehrhart and Sandler 1985). Most of the research on fraternities reports on samples of individual fraternity men. One group of studies compares the values, attitudes, perceptions, family socioeconomic status, psychological traits (aggressiveness, dependence), and so on, of fraternity and nonfraternity men (Bohrnstedt 1969; Fox, Hodge, and Ward 1987; Kanin 1967; Lemire 1979; Miller 1973). A second group attempts to identify the effects of fraternity membership over time on the values, attitudes, beliefs, or moral precepts of members (Hughes and Winston 1987; Marlowe and Auvenshine 1982; Miller 1973; Wilder, Hoyt, Doren, Hauck, and Zettle 1978; Wilder, Hoyt, Surbeck, Wilder, and Carney 1986). With minor exceptions, little research addresses the group and organizational context of fraternities or the social construction of fraternity life (for exceptions, see Letchworth 1969; Longino and Kart 1973; Smith 1964).

Gary Tash, writing as an alumnus and trial attorney in his fraternity's magazine, claims that over 90 percent of all gang rapes on college campuses involve fraternity men (1988, p. 2). Tash provides no evidence to substantiate this claim, but students of violence against women have been concerned with fraternity men's frequently reported involvement in rape episodes (Adams and Abarbanel 1988). Ehrhart and Sandler (1985) identify over 50 cases of gang rapes on campus perpetrated by fraternity men, and their analysis points to many of the conditions that we discuss here. Their analysis is unique in focusing on conditions in fraternities that make gang rapes of women by fraternity men both feasible and probable. They identify excessive alcohol use, isolation from external monitoring, treatment of women as prey, use of pornography, approval of violence, and excessive concern with competition as precipitating conditions to gang rape (also see Merton 1985; Roark 1987).

The study reported here confirmed and complemented these findings by focusing on both conditions and processes. We examined dynamics associated with the social construction of fraternity life, with a focus on processes that foster the use of coercion, including rape, in fraternity men's relations with women. Our examination of men's social fraternities on college and university campuses as groups and organizations led us to conclude that fraternities are a physical and sociocultural context that encourages the sexual coercion of women. We make no claims that all fraternities are "bad" or that all fraternity men are rapists. Our observations indicated, however, that rape is especially probable in fraternities because of the kinds of organizations they are, the kinds of members they have, the practices their members engage in, and a virtual absence of university or community oversight. Analyses that lay blame for rapes by fraternity men on "peer pressure" are, we feel, overly simplistic (cf. Burkhart 1989; Walsh 1989). We suggest, rather, that fraternities create a sociocultural context in which the use of coercion in sexual relations with women is nor-

mative and in which the mechanisms to keep this pattern of behavior in check are minimal at best and absent at worst. We conclude that unless fraternities change in fundamental ways, little improvement can be expected.

Methodology

Our goal was to analyze the group and organizational practices and conditions that create in fraternities an abusive social context for women. We developed a conceptual framework from an initial case study of an alleged gang rape at Florida State University that involved four fraternity men and an 18-year-old coed. The group rape took place on the third floor of a fraternity house and ended with the "dumping" of the woman in the hallway of a neighboring fraternity house. According to newspaper accounts, the victim's blood-alcohol concentration, when she was discovered, was .349 percent, more than three times the legal limit for automobile driving and an almost lethal amount. One law enforcement officer reported that sexual intercourse occurred during the time the victim was unconscious: "She was in a life-threatening situation" (*Tallahassee Democrat*, 1988b). When the victim was found, she was comatose and had suffered multiple scratches and abrasions. Crude words and a fraternity symbol had been written on her thighs (*Tampa Tribune*, 1988). When law enforcement officials tried to investigate the case, fraternity members refused to cooperate. This led, eventually, to a five-year ban of the fraternity from campus by the university and by the fraternity's national organization.

In trying to understand how such an event could have occurred, and how a group of over 150 members (exact figures are unknown because the fraternity refused to provide a membership roster) could hold rank, deny knowledge of the event, and allegedly lie to a grand jury, we analyzed newspaper articles about the case and conducted open-ended interviews with a variety of respondents about the case and about fraternities, rapes, alcohol use, gender relations, and sexual activities on campus. Our data included over 100 newspaper articles on the initial gang rape case; open-ended interviews with Greek (social fraternity and sorority) and non-Greek (independent) students (N = 20); university administrators (N = 8, five men, three women); and alumni advisers to Greek organizations (N = 6). Open-ended interviews were held also with judges, public and private defense attorneys, victim advocates, and state prosecutors regarding the processing of sexual assault cases. Data were analyzed using the grounded theory method (Glaser 1978; Martin and Turner 1986). In the following analysis, concepts generated from the data analysis are integrated with the literature on men's social fraternities, sexual coercion, and related issues.

Fraternities and the Social Construction of Men and Masculinity

Our research indicated that fraternities are vitally concerned—more than with anything else—with masculinity (cf. Kanin 1967). They work hard to create a macho image and context and try to avoid any suggestion of "wimpishness," effeminacy, and homosexuality. Valued members display, or are willing to go along with, a narrow conception of masculinity that stresses competition, athleticism, dominance, winning, conflict, wealth, material possessions, willingness to drink alcohol, and sexual prowess vis-a-vis women.

Valued Qualities of Members

When fraternity members talked about the kind of pledges they prefer, a litany of stereotypical and narrowly masculine attributes and behaviors was recited and feminine or woman-associated qualities and behaviors were expressly denounced (cf. Merton 1985). Fraternities seek men who are "athletic," "big guys," good in intramural competition, "who can talk college sports." Males "who

are willing to drink alcohol," "who drink socially," or "who can hold their liquor" are sought. Alcohol and activities associated with the recreational use of alcohol are cornerstones of fraternity social life. Nondrinkers are viewed with skepticism and rarely selected for membership.[1]

Fraternities try to avoid "geeks," nerds, and men said to give the fraternity a "wimpy" or "gay" reputation. Art, music, and humanities majors, majors in traditional women's fields (nursing, home economics, social work, education), men with long hair, and those whose appearance or dress violate current norms are rejected. Clean-cut, handsome men who dress well (are clean, neat, conforming, fashionable) are preferred. One sorority woman commented that "the top ranking fraternities have the best looking guys."

One fraternity man, a senior, said his fraternity recruited "some big guys, very athletic" over a two-year period to help overcome its image of wimpiness. His fraternity had won the interfraternity competition for highest grade-point average several years running but was looked down on as "wimpy, dancy, even gay." With their bigger, more athletic recruits, "our reputation improved; we're a much more recognized fraternity now." Thus a fraternity's reputation and status depends on members' possession of stereotypically masculine qualities. Good grades, campus leadership, and community service are "nice" but masculinity dominance—for example, in athletic events, physical size of members, athleticism of members—counts most.

Certain social skills are valued. Men are sought who "have good personalities," are friendly, and "have the ability to relate to girls" (cf. Longino and Kart 1973). One fraternity man, a junior, said: "We watch a guy [a potential pledge] talk to women . . . we want guys who can relate to girls." Assessing a pledge's ability to talk to women is, in part, a preoccupation with homosexuality and a conscious avoidance of men who seem to have effeminate manners or qualities. If a member is suspected of being gay, he is ostracized and informally drummed out of the fraternity. A fraternity with a reputation as wimpy or tolerant of gays is ridiculed and shunned by other fraternities. Militant heterosexuality is frequently used by men as a strategy to keep each other in line (Kimmel 1987).

Financial affluence or wealth, a male-associated value in American culture, is highly valued by fraternities. In accounting for why the fraternity involved in the gang rape that precipitated our research project had been recognized recently as "the best fraternity chapter in the United States," a university official said: "They were good-looking, a big fraternity, had lots of BMWs [expensive, German-made automobiles]." After the rape, newspaper stories described the fraternity members' affluence, noting the high number of members who owned expensive cars (*St. Petersburg Times*, 1988).

The Status and Norms of Pledgeship

A pledge (sometimes called an associate member) is a new recruit who occupies a trial membership status for a specific period of time. The pledge period (typically ranging from 10 to 15 weeks) gives fraternity brothers an opportunity to assess and socialize new recruits. Pledges evaluate the fraternity also and decide if they want to become brothers. The socialization experience is structured partly through assignment of a Big Brother to each pledge. Big Brothers are expected to teach pledges how to become a brother and to support them as they progress through the trial membership period. Some pledges are repelled by the pledging experience, which can entail physical abuse; harsh discipline; and demands to be subordinate, follow orders, and engage in demeaning routines and activities, similar to those used by the military to "make men out of boys" during boot camp.

Characteristics of the pledge experience are rationalized by fraternity members as necessary to help pledges unite into a group, rely on each other, and join together against outsiders. The process is highly masculinist in execution as well

as conception. A willingness to submit to authority, follow orders, and do as one is told is viewed as a sign of loyalty, togetherness, and unity. Fraternity pledges who find the pledge process offensive often drop out. Some do this by openly quitting, which can subject them to ridicule by brothers and other pledges, or they may deliberately fail to make the grades necessary for initiation or transfer schools and decline to reaffiliate with the fraternity on the new campus. One fraternity pledge who quit the fraternity he had pledged described an experience during pledgeship as follows:

This one guy was always picking on me. No matter what I did, I was wrong. One night after dinner, he and two other guys called me and two other pledges into the chapter room. He said, "Here X hold this 25 pound bag of ice at arms' length 'til I tell you to stop." I did it even though my arms and hands were killing me. When I asked if I could stop he grabbed me around the throat and lifted me off the floor. I thought he would choke me to death. He cussed me and called me all kinds of names. He took one of my fingers and twisted it until it nearly broke. . . . I stayed in the fraternity for a few more days but then I decided to quit. I hated it. Those guys are sick. They like seeing you suffer.

Fraternities' emphasis on toughness, withstanding pain and humiliation, obedience to superiors, and using physical force to obtain compliance contributes to an interpersonal style that de-emphasizes caring and sensitivity but fosters intragroup trust and loyalty. If the least macho or most critical pledges drop out, those who remain may be more receptive to, and influenced by, masculinist values and practices that encourage the use of force in sexual relations with women and the covering up of such behavior (cf. Kanin 1967).

Norms and Dynamics of Brotherhood

Brother is the status occupied by fraternity men to indicate their relations to each other and their membership in a particular fraternity organization or group. Brother is a male-specific status; only males can become brothers, although women can become "Little Sisters," a form of pseudomembership. "Becoming a brother" is a rite of passage that follows the consistent and often lengthy display by pledges of appropriately masculine qualities and behaviors. Brothers have a quasi-familial relationship with each other, are normatively said to share bonds of closeness and support, and are sharply set off from nonmembers. Brotherhood is a loosely defined term used to represent the bonds that develop among fraternity members and the obligations and expectations incumbent upon them (cf. Marlowe and Auvenshine [1982] on fraternities' failure to encourage "moral development" in freshman pledges).

Some of our respondents talked about brotherhood in almost reverential terms, viewing it as the most valuable benefit of fraternity membership. One senior, a business-school major who had been affiliated with a fairly high-status fraternity throughout four years on campus, said:

Brotherhood spurs friendship for life, which I consider its best aspect, although I didn't see it that way when I joined. Brotherhood bonds and unites. It instills values of caring about one another, caring about community, caring about ourselves. The values and bonds [of brotherhood] continually develop over the four years [in college] while normal friendships come and go.

Despite this idealization, most aspects of fraternity practice and conception are more mundane. Brotherhood often plays itself out as an overriding concern with masculinity and, by extension, femininity. As a consequence, fraternities comprise collectivities of highly masculinized men with attitudinal qualities and behavioral norms that predispose them to sexual coercion of women (cf. Kanin 1967; Merton 1985; Rapaport and Burkhart 1984). The norms of masculinity are complemented by conceptions of women and femininity that are equally distorted and stereotyped and that may enhance the probability of women's exploitation (cf. Ehrhart and Sandler 1985; Sanday 1981, 1986).

Practices of Brotherhood

Practices associated with fraternity brotherhood that contribute to the sexual coercion of women include a preoccupation with loyalty, group protection and secrecy, use of alcohol as a weapon, involvement in violence and physical force, and an emphasis on competition and superiority.

Loyalty, group protection, and secrecy. Loyalty is a fraternity preoccupation. Members are reminded constantly to be loyal to the fraternity and to their brothers. Among other ways, loyalty is played out in the practices of group protection and secrecy. The fraternity must be shielded from criticism. Members are admonished to avoid getting the fraternity in trouble and to bring all problems "to the chapter" (local branch of a national social fraternity) rather than to outsiders. Fraternities try to protect themselves from close scrutiny and criticism by the Interfraternity Council (a quasi-governing body composed of representatives from all social fraternities on campus), their fraternity's national office, university officials, law enforcement, the media, and the public. Protection of the fraternity often takes precedence over what is procedurally, ethically, or legally correct. Numerous examples were related to us of fraternity brothers' lying to outsiders to "protect the fraternity."

Group protection was observed in the alleged gang rape case with which we began our study. Except for one brother, a rapist who turned state's evidence, the entire remaining fraternity membership was accused by university and criminal justice officials of lying to protect the fraternity. Members consistently failed to cooperate even though the alleged crimes were felonies, involved only four men (two of whom were not even members of the local chapter), and the victim of the crime nearly died. According to a grand jury's findings, fraternity officers repeatedly broke appointments with law enforcement officials, refused to provide police with a list of members, and refused to cooperate with police and prosecutors investigating the case (*Florida Flambeau*, 1988).

Secrecy is a priority value and practice in fraternities, partly because full-fledged membership is premised on it (for confirmation, see Ehrhart and Sandler 1985; Longino and Kart 1973; Roark 1987). Secrecy is also a boundary-maintaining mechanism, demarcating in-group from out-group, us from them. Secret rituals, handshakes, and mottoes are revealed to pledge brothers as they are initiated into full brotherhood. Since only brothers are supposed to know a fraternity's secrets, such knowledge affirms membership in the fraternity and separates a brother from others. Extending secrecy tactics from protection of private knowledge to protection of the fraternity from criticism is a predictable development. Our interviews indicated that individual members knew the difference between right and wrong, but fraternity norms that emphasize loyalty, group protection, and secrecy often overrode standards of ethical correctness.

Alcohol as weapon. Alcohol use by fraternity men is normative. They use it on weekdays to relax after class and on weekends to "get drunk," "get crazy," and "get laid." The use of alcohol to obtain sex from women is pervasive—in other words, it is used as a weapon against sexual reluctance. According to several fraternity men whom we interviewed, alcohol is the major tool used to gain sexual mastery over women (cf. Adams and Abarbanel 1988; Ehrhart and Sandler 1985). One fraternity man, a 21-year-old senior, described alcohol use to gain sex as follows: "There are girls that you know will fuck, then some you have to put some effort into it. . . . You have to buy them drinks or find out if she's drunk enough. . . ."

A similar strategy is used collectively. A fraternity man said that at parties with Little Sisters: "We provide them with 'hunch punch' and things get wild. We get them drunk and most of the guys end up with one." "'Hunch punch,'" he said, "is a girls' drink made up of overproof alcohol and powdered Kool-Aid, no water or anything, just

ice. It's very strong. Two cups will do a number on a female." He had plans in the next academic term to surreptitiously give hunch punch to women in a "prim and proper" sorority because "having sex with prim and proper sorority girls is definitely a goal." These women are a challenge because they "won't openly consume alcohol and won't get openly drunk as hell." Their sororities have "standards committees" that forbid heavy drinking and easy sex.

In the gang rape case, our sources said that many fraternity men on campus believed the victim had a drinking problem and was thus an "easy make." According to newspaper accounts, she had been drinking alcohol on the evening she was raped; the lead assailant is alleged to have given her a bottle of wine after she arrived at his fraternity house. Portions of the rape occurred in a shower, and the victim was reportedly so drunk that her assailants had difficulty holding her in a standing position (*Tallahassee Democrat*, 1988a). While raping her, her assailants repeatedly told her they were members of another fraternity under the apparent belief that she was too drunk to know the difference. Of course, if she was too drunk to know who they were, she was too drunk to consent to sex (cf. Allgeier 1986; Tash 1988).

One respondent told us that gang rapes are wrong and can get one expelled, but he seemed to see nothing wrong in sexual coercion one-on-one. He seemed unaware that the use of alcohol to obtain sex from a woman is grounds for a claim that a rape occurred (cf. Tash 1988). Few women on campus (who also may not know these grounds) report date rapes, however; so the odds of detection and punishment are slim for fraternity men who use alcohol for "seduction" purposes (cf. Byington and Keeter 1988; Merton 1985).

Violence and physical force. Fraternity men have a history of violence (Ehrhart and Sandler 1985; Roark 1987). Their record of hazing, fighting, property destruction, and rape has caused them problems with insurance companies (Bradford 1986; Pressley 1987). Two university officials told us that fraternities "are the third riskiest property to insure behind toxic waste dumps and amusement parks." Fraternities are increasingly defendants in legal actions brought by pledges subjected to hazing (Meyer 1986; Pressley 1987) and by women who were raped by one or more members. In a recent alleged gang rape incident at another Florida university, prosecutors failed to file charges but the victim filed a civil suit against the fraternity nevertheless (*Tallahassee Democrat*, 1989).

Competition and superiority. Interfraternity rivalry fosters in-group identification and out-group hostility. Fraternities stress pride of membership and superiority over other fraternities as major goals. Interfraternity rivalries take many forms, including competition for desirable pledges, size of pledge class, size of membership, size and appearance of fraternity house, superiority in intramural sports, highest grade-point averages, giving the best parties, gaining the best or most campus leadership roles, and, of great importance, attracting and displaying "good looking women." Rivalry is particularly intense over members, intramural sports, and women (cf. Messner 1989).

Fraternities' Commodification of Women

In claiming that women are treated by fraternities as commodities, we mean that fraternities knowingly, and intentionally, *use* women for their benefit. Fraternities use women as bait for new members, as servers of brother's needs, and as sexual prey.

Women as bait. Fashionably attractive women help a fraternity attract new members. As one fraternity man, a junior, said, "They are good bait." Beautiful, sociable women are believed to impress the right kind of pledges and give the impression that the fraternity can deliver this type of woman to its members. Photographs of shapely, attractive coeds are printed in fraternity brochures and videotapes that are distributed and shown to potential pledges. The women pictured are often dressed in bikinis, at the beach, and are pictured hugging the brothers of the fraternity. One university official says such recruitment materials give the message: "Hey, they're here for you, you can have whatever you want," and, "we have the best looking women. Join us and you can have them too." Another commented: "Something's wrong when males join an all-male organization as the best place to meet women. It's so illogical."

Fraternities compete in promising access to beautiful women. One fraternity man, a senior, commented that "the attraction of girls [i.e., a fraternity's success in attracting women] is a big status symbol for fraternities." One university official commented that the use of women as a recruiting tool is so well entrenched that fraternities that might be willing to forgo it say they cannot afford to unless other fraternities do so as well. One fraternity man said, "Look, if we don't have Little Sisters, the fraternities that do will get all the good pledges." Another said, "We won't have as good a rush [the period during which new members are assessed and selected] if we don't have these women around."

In displaying good-looking, attractive, skimpily dressed, nubile women to potential members, fraternities implicitly, and sometimes explicitly, promise sexual access to women. One fraternity man commented that "part of what being in a fraternity is all about is the sex" and explained how his fraternity uses Little Sisters to recruit new members:

We'll tell the sweetheart [the fraternity's term for Little Sister], "You're gorgeous; you can get him." We'll tell her to fake a scam and she'll go hang all over him during a rush party, kiss him, and he thinks he's done wonderful and wants to join. The girls think it's great too. It's flattering for them.

Women as servers. The use of women as servers is exemplified in the Little Sister program. Little

Sisters are undergraduate women who are rushed and selected in a manner parallel to the recruitment of fraternity men. They are affiliated with the fraternity in a formal but unofficial way and are able, indeed required, to wear the fraternity's Greek letters. Little Sisters are not full-fledged fraternity members, however; and fraternity national offices and most universities do not register or regulate them. Each fraternity has an officer called Little Sister Chairman who oversees their organization and activities. The Little Sisters elect officers among themselves, pay monthly dues to the fraternity, and have well-defined roles. Their dues are used to pay for the fraternity's social events, and Little Sisters are expected to attend and hostess fraternity parties and hang around the house to make it a "nice place to be." One fraternity man, a senior, described Little Sisters this way: "They are very social girls, willing to join in, be affiliated with the group, devoted to the fraternity." Another member, a sophomore, said: "Their sole purpose is social—attend parties, attract new members, and 'take care' of the guys."

Our observations and interviews suggested that women selected by fraternities as Little Sisters are physically attractive, possess good social skills, and are willing to devote time and energy to the fraternity and its members.

One undergraduate woman gave the following job description for Little Sisters to a campus newspaper:

It's not just making appearances at all the parties but entails many more responsibilities. You're going to be expected to go to all the intramural games to cheer the brothers on, support and encourage the pledges, and just be around to bring some extra life to the house. [As a Little Sister] you have to agree to take on a new responsibility other than studying to maintain your grades and managing to keep your checkbook from bouncing. You have to make time to be a part of the fraternity and support the brothers in all they do. (The Tomahawk, 1988)

The title of Little Sister reflects women's subordinate status; fraternity men in a parallel role are called Big Brothers. Big Brothers assist a sorority primarily with the physical work of sorority rushes, which, compared to fraternity rushes, are more formal, structured, and intensive. Sorority rushes take place in the daytime and fraternity rushes at night so fraternity men are free to help. According to one fraternity member, Little Sister status is a benefit to women because it gives them a social outlet and "the protection of the brothers." The gender-stereotypic conceptions and obligations of these Little Sister and Big Brother statuses indicate that fraternities and sororities promote a gender hierarchy on campus that fosters subordination and dependence in women, thus encouraging sexual exploitation and the belief that it is acceptable.

Women as sexual prey. Little Sisters are a sexual utility. Many Little Sisters do not belong to sororities and lack peer support for refraining from unwanted sexual relations. One fraternity man (whose fraternity has 65 members and 85 Little Sisters) told us they had recruited "wholesale" in the prior year to "get lots of new women." The structural access to women that the Little Sister program provides and the absence of normative supports for refusing fraternity members' sexual advances may make women in this program particularly susceptible to coerced sexual encounters with fraternity men.

Access to women for sexual gratification is a presumed benefit of fraternity membership, promised in recruitment materials and strategies and through brothers' conversations with new recruits. One fraternity man said: "We always tell the guys that you get sex all the time, there's always new girls. . . . After I became a Greek, I found out I could be with females at will." A university official told us that, based on his observations, "no one [i.e., fraternity men] on this campus wants to have 'relationships.' They just want to have fun [i.e., sex]." Fraternity men plan and execute strategies aimed at obtaining sexual gratification, and this occurs at both individual and collective levels.

Individual strategies include getting a woman drunk and spending a great deal of money on her. As for collective strategies, most of our undergraduate interviewees agreed that fraternity parties often culminate in sex and that this outcome is planned. One fraternity man said fraternity parties often involve sex and nudity and can "turn into orgies." Orgies may be planned in advance, such as the Bowery Ball party held by one fraternity. A former fraternity member said of this party:

The entire idea behind this is sex. Both men and women come to the party wearing little or nothing. There are pornographic pinups on the walls and usually porno movies playing on the TV. The music carries sexual overtones. . . . They just get schnockered [drunk] and, in most cases, they also get laid.

When asked about the women who come to such a party, he said: "Some Little Sisters just won't go. . . . The girls who do are looking for a good time, girls who don't know what it is, things like that."

Other respondents denied that fraternity parties are orgies but said that sex is always talked about among the brothers and they all know "who each other is doing it with." One member said that most of the time, guys have sex with their girlfriends "but with socials, girlfriends aren't allowed to come and it's their [members'] big chance [to have sex with other women]." The use of alcohol to help them get women into bed is a routine strategy at fraternity parties.

Conclusions

In general, our research indicated that the organization and membership of fraternities contribute heavily to coercive and often violent sex. Fraternity houses are occupied by same-sex (all men) and same-age (late teens, early twenties) peers whose maturity and judgment is often less than ideal. Yet fraternity houses are private dwellings that are mostly off-limits to, and away from scrutiny of, university and community representatives, with the result that fraternity house events seldom come to the attention of outsiders. Practices associated with the social construction of fraternity brotherhood emphasize a macho conception of men and masculinity, a narrow, stereotyped conception of women and femininity, and the treatment of women as commodities. Other practices contributing to coercive sexual relations and the cover-up of rapes include excessive alcohol use, competitiveness, and normative support for deviance and secrecy (cf. Bogal-Allbritten and Allbritten 1985; Kanin 1967).

Some fraternity practices exacerbate others. Brotherhood norms require "sticking together" regardless of right or wrong; thus rape episodes are unlikely to be stopped or reported to outsiders, even when witnesses disapprove. The ability to use alcohol without scrutiny by authorities and alcohol's frequent association with violence, including sexual coercion, facilitates rape in fraternity houses. Fraternity norms that emphasize the value of maleness and masculinity over femaleness and femininity and that elevate the status of men and lower the status of women in members' eyes undermine perceptions and treatment of women as persons who deserve consideration and care (cf. Ehrhart and Sandler 1985; Merton 1985).

Androgynous men and men with a broad range of interests and attributes are lost to fraternities through their recruitment practices. Masculinity of a narrow and stereotypical type helps create attitudes, norms, and practices that predispose fraternity men to coerce women sexually, both individually and collectively (Allgeier 1986; Hood 1989; Sanday 1981, 1986). Male athletes on campus may be similarly disposed for the same reasons (Kirshenbaum 1989; Telander and Sullivan 1989).

Research into the social contexts in which rape crimes occur and the social constructions associated with these contexts illuminate rape dynamics on campus. Blanchard (1959) found that group rapes almost always have a leader who pushes others into the crime. He also found that the leader's latent homosexuality, desire to show off to his peers, or fear of failing to prove himself a man are frequently an impetus. Fraternity norms and practices contribute to the approval and use of sexual coercion as an accepted tactic in relations with women. Alcohol-induced compliance is normative, whereas, presumably, use of a knife, gun, or threat of bodily harm would not be because the woman who "drinks too much" is viewed as "causing her own rape" (cf. Ehrhart and Sandler 1985).

Our research led us to conclude that fraternity norms and practices influence members to view the sexual coercion of women, which is a felony crime, as sport, a contest, or a game (cf. Sato 1988). This sport is played not between men and women but between men and men. Women are the pawns or prey in the interfraternity rivalry game; they prove that a fraternity is successful or prestigious. The use of women in this way encourages fraternity men to see women as objects and sexual coercion as sport. Today's societal norms support young women's right to engage in sex at their discretion, and coercion is unnecessary in a mutually desired encounter. However, nubile young women say they prefer to be "in a relationship" to have sex while young men say they prefer to "get laid" without a commitment (Muehlenhard and Linton 1987). These differences may reflect, in part, American puritanism and men's fears of sexual intimacy or perhaps intimacy of any kind. In a fraternity context, getting sex without giving emotionally demonstrates "cool" masculinity. More important, it poses no threat to the bonding and loyalty of the fraternity brotherhood (cf. Farr 1988). Drinking large quantities of alcohol before having sex suggests that "scoring" rather than intrinsic sexual pleasure is a primary concern of fraternity men.

Unless fraternities' composition, goals, structures, and practices change in fundamental ways, women on campus will continue to be sexual prey for fraternity men. As all-male enclaves dedicated to opposing faculty and administration and to cementing in-group ties, fraternity members eschew any hint of homosexuality. Their version of masculinity transforms women, and men with wom-

anly characteristics, into the out-group. "Womanly men" are ostracized; feminine women are used to demonstrate members' masculinity. Encouraging renewed emphasis on their founding values (Longino and Kart 1973), service orientation and activities (Lemire 1979), or members' moral development (Marlowe and Auvenshine 1982) will have little effect on fraternities' treatment of women. A case for or against fraternities cannot be made by studying individual members. The fraternity qua group and origination is at issue. Located on campus along with many vulnerable women, embedded in a sexist society, and caught up in masculinist goals, practices, and values, fraternities' violation of women—including forcible rape—should come as no surprise.

Note

1. Recent bans by some universities on open-keg parties at fraternity houses have resulted in heavy drinking before coming to a party and an increase in drunkenness among those who attend. This may aggravate, rather than improve, the treatment of women by fraternity men at parties.

References

Allgeier, Elizabeth. 1986. "Coercive Versus Consensual Sexual Interactions." G. Stanley Hall Lecture to American Psychological Association Annual Meeting, Washington, DC, August.

Adams, Aileen and Gail Abarbanel. 1988. *Sexual Assault on Campus: What Colleges Can Do.* Santa Monica, CA: Rape Treatment Center.

Blanchard, W. H. 1959. "The Group Process in Gang Rape." *Journal of Social Psychology* 49:259-66.

Bogal-Allbritten, Rosemarie B. and William L. Allbritten. 1985. "The Hidden Victims: Courtship Violence Among College Students." *Journal of College Student Personnel* 43:201-4.

Bohrnstedt, George W. 1969. "Conservatism, Authoritarianism and Religiosity of Fraternity Pledges." *Journal of College Student Personnel* 27: 36-43 .

Bradford, Michael. 1986. "Tight Market Dries Up Nightlife at University." *Business Insurance* (March 2): 2, 6.

Burkhart, Barry. 1989. Comments in Seminar on Acquaintance/Date Rape Prevention: A National Video Teleconference, February 2.

Burkhart, Barry R. and Annette L. Stanton. 1985. "Sexual Aggression in Acquaintance Relationships." Pp. 43-65 in *Violence in Intimate Relationships*, edited by G. Russell. Englewood Cliffs, NJ: Spectrum.

Byington, Diane B. and Karen W. Keeter. 1988. "Assessing Needs of Sexual Assault Victims on a University Campus." Pp. 23-31 in *Student Services: Responding to Issues and Challenges.* Chapel Hill: University of North Carolina Press.

Chancer, Lynn S. 1987. "New Bedford, Massachusetts, March 6, 1983-March 22, 1984: The 'Before and After' of a Group Rape." *Gender & Society* 1:239-60.

Ehrhart, Julie K. and Bernice R. Sandler. 1985. *Campus Gang Rape: Party Games?* Washington, DC: Association of American Colleges.

Farr, K. A. 1988. "Dominance Bonding Through the Good Old Boys Sociability Network." *Sex Roles* 18:259-77.

Florida Flambeau. 1988. "Pike Members Indicted in Rape." (May 19):1, 5.

Fox, Elaine, Charles Hodge, and Walter Ward. 1987. "A Comparison of Attitudes Held by Black and White Fraternity Members." *Journal of Negro Education* 56: 521-34.

Geis, Gilbert. 1971. "Group Sexual Assaults." *Medical Aspects of Human Sexuality* 5:101-13.

Glaser, Barney G. 1978. *Theoretical Sensitivity: Advances in the Methodology of Grounded Theory.* Mill Valley, CA: Sociology Press.

Hood, Jane. 1989. "Why Our Society Is Rape-Prone." *New York Times*, May 16.

Hughes, Michael J. and Roger B. Winston, Jr. 1987. "Effects of Fraternity Membership on Interpersonal Values." *Journal of College Student Personnel* 45:405-11.

Kanin, Eugene J. 1967. "Reference Groups and Sex Conduct Norm Violations." *The Sociological Quarterly* 8:495-504.

Kimmel, Michael, ed. 1987. *Changing Men: New Directions in Research on Men and Masculinity.* Newbury Park, CA: Sage.

Kirshenbaum, Jerry. 1989. "Special Report, An American Disgrace: A Violent and Unprecedented Lawlessness Has Arisen Among College Athletes in all Parts of the Country." *Sports Illustrated* (February 27): 16-19.

Lemire, David. 1979. "One Investigation of the Stereotypes Associated with Fraternities and Sororities." *Journal of College Student Personnel* 37:54-57.

Letchworth, G. E. 1969. "Fraternities Now and in the Future." *Journal of College Student Personnel* 10:118-22.

Longino, Charles F., Jr., and Cary S. Kart. 1973. "The College Fraternity: An Assessment of Theory and Research." *Journal of College Student Personnel* 31:118-25.

Marlowe, Anne F. and Dwight C. Auvenshine. 1982. "Greek Membership: Its Impact on the Moral Development of College Freshmen." *Journal of College Student Personnel* 40:53–57.

Martin, Patricia Yancey and Barry A. Turner. 1986. "Grounded Theory and Organizational Research." *Journal of Applied Behavioral Science* 22:141–57.

Merton, Andrew. 1985. "On Competition and Class: Return to Brotherhood." *Ms.* (September): 60–65, 121–22.

Messner, Michael. 1989. "Masculinities and Athletic Careers." *Gender & Society* 3:71–88.

Meyer, T. J. 1986. "Fight Against Hazing Rituals Rages on Campuses." *Chronicle of Higher Education* (March 12):34–36.

Miller, Leonard D. 1973. "Distinctive Characteristics of Fraternity Members." *Journal of College Student Personnel* 31:126–28.

Muehlenhard, Charlene L. and Melaney A. Linton. 1987. "Date Rape and Sexual Aggression in Dating Situations: Incidence and Risk Factors." *Journal of Counseling Psychology* 34:186–96.

Pressley, Sue Anne. 1987. "Fraternity Hell Night Still Endures." *Washington Post* (August 11):B1.

Rapaport, Karen and Barry R. Burkhart. 1984. "Personality and Attitudinal Characteristics of Sexually Coercive College Males." *Journal of Abnormal Psychology* 93:216–21.

Roark, Mary L. 1987. "Preventing Violence on College Campuses." *Journal of Counseling and Development* 65:367–70.

Sanday, Peggy Reeves. 1981. "The Socio-Cultural Context of Rape: A Cross-Cultural Study." *Journal of Social Issues* 37:5–27.

———. 1986. "Rape and the Silencing of the Feminine." Pp. 84–101 in *Rape*, edited by S. Tomaselli and R. Porter. Oxford: Basil Blackwell.

St. Petersburg Times. 1988. "A Greek Tragedy." (May 29):1F, 6F.

Sato, Ikuya. 1988. "Play Theory of Delinquency: Toward a General Theory of 'Action.'" *Symbolic Interaction* 11:191–212.

Smith, T. 1964. "Emergence and Maintenance of Fraternal Solidarity." *Pacific Sociological Review* 7:29–37.

Tallahassee Democrat. 1988a. "FSU Fraternity Brothers Charged" (April 27):1A, 12A.

———. 1988b. "FSU Interviewing Students About Alleged Rape" (April 24):1D.

———.1989. "Woman Sues Stetson in Alleged Rape" (March 19):3B.

Tampa Tribune. 1988. "Fraternity Brothers Charged in Sexual Assault of FSU Coed." (April 27):6B.

Tash, Gary B. 1988. "Date Rape." *The Emerald of Sigma Pi Fraternity* 75(4):1-2.

Telander, Rick and Robert Sullivan. 1989. "Special Report, You Reap What You Sow." *Sports Illustrated* (February 27):20-34.

The Tomahawk. 1988. "A Look Back at Rush, A Mixture of Hard Work and Fun" (April/May): 3D.

Walsh, Claire. 1989. Comments in Seminar on Acquaintance/Date Rape Prevention: A National Video Teleconference, February 2.

Wilder, David H., Arlyne E. Hoyt, Dennis M. Doren, William E. Hauck, and Robert D. Zettle. 1978. "The Impact of Fraternity and Sorority Membership on Values and Attitudes." *Journal of College Student Personnel* 36:445-49.

Wilder, David H., Arlyne E. Hoyt, Beth Shuster Surbeck, Janet C. Wilder, and Patricia Imperatrice Carney. 1986. "Greek Affiliation and Attitude Change in College Students." *Journal of College Student Personnel* 44: 510-19.

Questions for Reflection

1. What is your personal reaction to this article? Which of the authors' analyses is most problematic to you?

2. Are there other types of groups whose cohesiveness also leads to similar actions and issues?

3. What other factors contribute to incidents of date and gang rape?

SELECTION EIGHT

This article was based on a nineteen-month ethnographic study. In it Dr. Melba Sánchez-Ayéndez examines how the characteristics of Puerto Rican culture influence the expectations that older women have about themselves and others who constitute their informal supportive networks. Gender expectations as well as other cultural imperatives are seen as affecting elderly women's sense of well being. The level of social support that is expected and received is understandable using this cultural framework. The article helps us think about and deal with inter-generational communication. Understanding what your parents and grand-parents expect and need from you can often be facilitated by examining their culture of origin.

Puerto Rican Elderly Women:
Shared Meanings and Informal Supportive Networks

Melba Sánchez-Ayéndez

Introduction

Studies of older adults' support systems have seldom taken into account how values within a specific cultural context affect expectations of support and patterns of assistance in social networks. Such networks and supportive relations have a cultural dimension reflecting a system of shared meanings. These meanings affect social interaction and the expectations people have of their relationships with others.

Ethnicity and gender affect a person's adjustment to old age. Although sharing a "minority" position produces similar consequences among members of different ethnic minority groups, the groups' diversity lies in their distinctive systems of shared meanings. Studies of older adults in eth-

nic minority groups have rarely focused on the cultural contents of ethnicity affecting the aging process, particularly of women (Barth 1969). Cultural value orientations are central to understanding how minority elders approach growing old and how they meet the physical and emotional changes associated with aging.

This article describes the interplay between values and behavior in family and community of a group of older Puerto Rican women living on low incomes in Boston.[1] It explores how values emphasizing family interdependence and different roles of women and men shape the women's expectations, behavior, and supportive familial and community networks.

Being a Woman Is Different from Being a Man

The women interviewed believe in a dual standard of conduct for men and women. This dual

From *All-American Women: Lines That Divide, Ties That Bind*, ed. Johnnetta B. Cole (New York: Free Press, 1986), 172–186. Reprinted by permission of The Free Press, an imprint of Simon & Schuster.

standard is apparent in different attributes assigned to women and men, roles expected of them, and authority exercised by them.

The principal role of men in the family is viewed as that of provider; their main responsibility is economic in nature. Although fathers are expected to be affectionate with their children, child care is not seen to be a man's responsibility. Men are not envisioned within the domestic sphere.

The "ideal" man must be the protector of the family, able to control his emotions and be self-sufficient. Men enjoy more freedom in the public world than do women. From the women's perspective, the ideal of maleness is linked to the concept of *machismo*. This concept assumes men have a stronger sexual drive than women, a need to prove virility by the conquest of women, a dominant position in relation to females, and a belligerent attitude when confronted by male peers.

The women see themselves as subordinate to men and recognize the preeminence of male authority. They believe women ought to be patient and largely forbearing in their relations with men, particularly male family members. Patience and forbearance, however, are not confused with passivity or total submissiveness. The elderly Puerto Rican women do not conceive of themselves or other women as "resigned females" but as dynamic beings, continually devising strategies to improve everyday situations within and outside the household.

Rosa Mendoza,[2] now sixty-five, feels no regrets for having decided at thirty years of age and after nine years of marriage not to put up with her husband's heavy drinking any longer. She moved out of her house and went to live with her mother.

I was patient for many years. I put up with his drunkenness and worked hard to earn money One day I decided I'd be better off without him. One thing is to be patient, and another to be a complete fool. So I moved out.

Although conscious of their subordinate status to their husbands, wives are also aware of their power and the demands they can make. Ana Fuentes recalls when her husband had a mistress. Ana was thirty-eight.

I knew he had a mistress in a nearby town. I was patient for a long time, hoping it would end. Most men, sooner or later, have a mistress somewhere. But when it didn't end after quite a time and everyone in the neighborhood knew about it, I said "I am fed up!" He came home one evening and the things I told him! I even said I'd go to that woman's house and beat her if I had to. . . . He knew I was not bluffing; that this was not just another argument. He tried to answer back and I didn't let him. He remained silent. . . . And you know what? He stopped seeing her! A woman can endure many things for a long time, but the time comes when she has to defend her rights.

These older Puerto Rican women perceive the home as the center around which the female world revolves. Home is the woman's domain; women generally make decisions about household maintenance and men seldom intervene.

Family relations are considered part of the domestic sphere and therefore a female responsibility. The women believe that success in marriage depends on the woman's ability to "make the marriage work."

A marriage lasts as long as the woman decides it will last. It is us who make a marriage work, who put up with things, who try to make ends meet, who yield.

The norm of female subordination is evident in the view that marriage will last as long as the woman "puts up with things" and deals with marriage from her subordinate status. Good relations with affinal kin are also a woman's responsibility. They are perceived as relations between the wife's domestic unit and other women's domestic units.

Motherhood

Motherhood is seen by these older Puerto Rican women as the central role of women. Their concept of motherhood is based on the female capacity to bear children and on the notion of *marianismo*, which presents the Virgin Mary as a role model (Stevens 1973). *Marianismo* presupposes that it is through motherhood that a woman realizes herself and derives her life's greatest satisfactions.

A woman's reproductive role is viewed as leading her toward more commitment to and a better understanding of her children than is shown by the father. One of the women emphasized this view:

It is easier for a man to leave his children and form a new home with another woman, or not to be as forgiving of children as a mother is. They will never know what it is like to carry a child inside, feel it growing, and then bring that child into the world. This is why a mother is always willing to forgive and make sacrifices. That creature is part of you; it nourished from you and came from within you. But it is not so for men. To them, a child is a being they receive once it is born. The attachment can never be the same.

The view that childrearing is their main responsibility in life comes from this conceptualization of the mother-child bond. For the older women, raising children means more than looking after the needs of offspring. It involves being able to offer them every possible opportunity for a better life, during childhood or adulthood, even if this requires personal sacrifices.

As mother and head of the domestic domain, a woman is also responsible for establishing the bases for close and good relations among her children. From childhood through adulthood, the creation and maintenance of family unity among offspring is considered another female responsibility.

Family Unity and Interdependence

Family Unity

Ideal family relations are seen as based on two interrelated themes, family unity and family interdependence. Family unity refers to the desirability of close and intimate kin ties, with members getting along well and keeping in frequent contact despite dispersal.

Celebration of holidays and special occasions are seen as opportunities for kin to be together and strengthen family ties. Family members, particularly grandparents, adult children, and grandchildren, are often reunited at Christmas, New Year's, Mother's and Father's days, Easter, and Thanksgiving. Special celebrations like weddings, baptisms, first communions, birthdays, graduations, and funerals occasion reunions with other family members. Whether to celebrate happy or sad events, the older women encourage family gatherings as a way of strengthening kinship ties and fostering family continuity.

The value the women place on family unity is also evident in their desire for frequent interaction with kin members. Visits and telephone calls demonstrate a caring attitude by family members which cements family unity.

Family unity is viewed as contributing to the strengthening of family interdependence. Many of the older women repeat a proverb when referring to family unity: *En la unión está la fuerza.* ("In union there is strength.") They believe that the greater the degree of unity in the family, the greater the emphasis family members will place on interdependence and familial obligation.

Family Interdependence

Despite adaptation to life in a culturally different society, Puerto Rican families in the United States are still defined by strong norms of reciprocity among family members, especially those in the immediate kinship group (Cantor 1979; Carrasquillo 1982; Delgado 1981; Donaldson and Martinez 1980; Sánchez-Ayéndez 1984). Interdependence within the Puerto Rican symbolic framework "fits an orientation to life that stresses that the individual is not capable of doing everything and doing it well. Therefore, he should rely on others for assistance" (Bastida 1979: 70). Individualism and self-reliance assume a different meaning from the one prevailing in the dominant U.S. cultural tradition. Individuals in Puerto Rican families will expect and ask for assistance from certain people in their social networks without any derogatory implications for self-esteem.

Family interdependence is a value to which these older Puerto Rican women strongly adhere.

It influences patterns of mutual assistance with their children as well as expectations of support. The older women expect to be taken care of during old age by their adult children. The notion of filial duty ensues from the value orientation of interdependence. Adult children are understood to have a responsibility toward their aged parents in exchange for the functions that parents performed for them throughout their upbringing. Expected reciprocity from offspring is intertwined with the concept of filial love and the nature of the parent-child relationship.

Parental duties of childrearing are perceived as inherent in the "parent" role and also lay the basis for long-term reciprocity with children, particularly during old age. The centrality that motherhood has in the lives of the older women contributes to creating great expectations among them of reciprocity from children. More elderly women than men verbalize disappointment when one of their children does not participate in the expected interdependence ties. Disappointment is unlikely to arise when an adult child cannot help due to financial or personal reasons. However, it is bound to arise when a child chooses not to assist the older parent for other reasons.

These older Puerto Rican women stress that good offspring ought to help their parents, contingent upon available resources. Statements such as the following are common:

Of course I go to my children when I have a problem! To whom would I turn? I raised them and worked very hard to give them the little I could. Now that I am old, they try to help me in whatever they can. . . . Good offspring should help their aged parents as much as they are able to.

Interdependence for Puerto Rican older parents also means helping their children and grandchildren. Many times they provide help when it is not explicitly requested. They are happy when they can perform supportive tasks for their children's families. The child who needs help, no matter how old, is not judged as dependent or a failure.

Reciprocity is not based on strictly equal exchanges. Due to the rapid pace of life, lack of financial resources, or personal problems, adult children are not always able to provide the care the elder parent needs. Many times, the older adults provide their families with more financial and instrumental assistance than their children are able to provide them. Of utmost importance to the older women is not that their children be able to help all the time, but that they visit or call frequently. They place more emphasis on emotional support from their offspring than on any other form of support.

Gloria Santos, for example, has a son and a daughter. While they do not live in the same state as their mother, they each send her fifty to seventy dollars every month. Yet, she is disappointed with her children and explains why:

They both have good salaries but call me only once or twice a month. I hardly know my grandchildren. All I ask from them is that they be closer to me, that they visit and call me more often. They only visit me once a year and only for one or two days. I've told my daughter that instead of sending me money she could call me more often. I was a good mother and worked hard in order for them to get a good education and have everything. All I expected from them was to show me they care, that they love me.

The importance that the older women attach to family interdependence does not imply that they constantly require assistance from children or that they do not value their independence. They prefer to live in their own households rather than with their adult children. They also try to solve as many problems as possible by themselves. But when support is needed, the adult children are expected to assist the aged parent to the degree they are able. This does not engender conflict or lowered self-esteem for the aged adult. Conflict and dissatisfaction are caused when adult children do not offer any support at all.

Sex Roles and Familial Supportive Networks

The family is the predominant source of support for most of these older women, providing instrumental and emotional support in daily life as well as assistance during health crises or times of need. Adult children play a central role in providing familial support to old parents. For married women, husbands are also an important component of their support system. At the same time, most of the older women still perform functional roles for their families.

Support from Adult Children

The support and helpfulness expected from offspring is related to perceptions of the difference between men and women. Older women seek different types of assistance from daughters than from sons. Daughters are perceived as being inherently better able to understand their mothers due to their shared status and qualities as women; they are also considered more reliable. Sons are not expected to help as much as daughters or in the same way. When a daughter does not fulfill the obligations expected of her, complaints are more bitter than if the same were true of a son: "Men are different; they do not feel as we feel. But she is a woman; she should know better." Daughters are also expected to visit and/or call more frequently than are sons. As women are linked closely to the domestic domain, they are held responsible for the care of family relations. Motherhood is perceived as creating an emotional bond among women. When daughters become mothers, the older women anticipate stronger ties and more support from them.

Once a daughter experiences motherhood, she understands the suffering and hardships you underwent for her. Sons will never be able to understand this.

My daughter always helped me. But when she became a mother for the first time, she grew much closer to me. It was then when she was able to understand how much a mother can love.

Most of the older women go to a daughter first when confronted by an emotional problem. Daughters are felt to be more patient and better able to understand them as women. It is not that older women never discuss their emotional problems with their sons, but they prefer to discuss them with their daughters. For example, Juana

Rivera has two sons who live in the same city as she and a daughter who resides in Puerto Rico. She and her sons get along well and see each other often. The sons stop by their mother's house every day after work, talk about daily happenings, and assist her with some tasks. However, when a physical exam revealed a breast tumor thought to be malignant, it was to her daughter in Puerto Rico that the old woman expressed her worries. She recalls that time of crisis:

Eddie was with me when the doctor told me of the possibility of a tumor. I was brave. I didn't want him to see me upset. They [sons] get nervous when I get upset or cry. . . . That evening I called my daughter and talked to her. . . . She was very understanding and comforted me. I can always depend on her to understand me. She is the person who better understands me. My sons are also understanding, but she is a woman and understands more.

Although adult children are sources of assistance during the illnesses of their mothers, it is generally daughters from whom more is expected. Quite often daughters take their sick parents into their homes or stay overnight in the parental household in order to provide better care. Sons, as well as daughters, take the aged parent to the hospital or doctors' offices and buy medicines if necessary. However, it is more often daughters who check on their parents, provide care, and perform household chores when the parent is sick.

When the old women have been hospitalized, adult children living nearby tend to visit the hospital daily. Daughters and daughters-in-law sometimes cook special meals for the sick parent and bring the meals to the hospital. Quite often, adult children living in other states or in Puerto Rico come to help care for the aged parent or be present at the time of an operation. When Juana Rivera had exploratory surgery on her breast, her daughter came from Puerto Rico and stayed with her mother throughout the convalescence. Similarly, when Ana Toledo suffered a stroke and remained unconscious for four days, three of her six children residing in other states came to be with her and their siblings. After her release from the hospital, a daughter from New Jersey stayed at her mother's house for a week. When she left, the children who live near the old woman took turns looking after her.

Most adult children are also helpful in assisting with chores of daily living. At times, offspring take their widowed mothers grocery shopping. Other times, the older women give their children money to do the shopping for them. Daughters are more often asked to do these favors and to also buy personal care items and clothes for their mothers. Some adult offspring also assist by depositing Social Security checks, checking post office boxes, and buying money orders.

Support from Elderly Mothers

The Puerto Rican older women play an active role in providing assistance to their adult children. Gender affects the frequency of emotional support offered as well as the dynamics of the support. The older women offer advice more often to daughters than to sons on matters related to childrearing. And the approach used differs according to the children's gender. For example, one older woman stated,

I never ask my son openly what is wrong with him. I do not want him to think that I believe he needs help to solve his problems; he is a man. . . . Yet, as a mother I worry. It is my duty to listen and offer him advice. With my daughter it is different; I can be more direct. She doesn't have to prove to me that she is self-sufficient.

Another woman expressed similar views:

Of course I give advice to my sons! When they have had problems with their wives, their children, even among themselves, I listen to them, and tell them what I think. But with my daughters I am more open. You see, if I ask one of my sons what is wrong and he doesn't want to tell me, I don't insist too much; I'll ask later, maybe in a different way; and they will tell me sooner or later. With my daughters, if they don't want to tell me, I insist. They know I am a mother and a woman like them and that I can understand.

Older mothers perceive sons and daughters as in equal need of support. Daughters, however, are understood to face additional problems in areas such as conjugal relations, childrearing, and sexual harassment, due to their status as women.

Emotional support to daughters-in-law is also offered, particularly when they are encountering marriage or childrearing problems. Josefina Montes explains the active role she played in comforting her daughter-in-law, whose husband was having an extramarital affair:

I told her not to give up, that she had to defend what was hers. I always listened to her and tried to offer some comfort. . . . When my son would come to my home to visit I would ask him "What is wrong with you? Don't you realize what a good mother and wife that woman is?". . . . I made it my business that he did not forget the exceptional woman she is. . . . I told him I didn't want to ever see him with the other one and not to mention her name in front of me. . . . I was on his case for almost two years. . . . All the time I told her to be patient. . . . It took time but he finally broke up with the other one.

When relations between mother and daughters-in-law are not friendly, support is not usually present. Eulalia Valle says that when her son left his wife and children to move in with another woman, there was not much she could do for her daughter-in-law.

There was not much I could do. What could I tell him? I couldn't say she was nice to me. . . . Once I tried to make him see how much she was hurting and he replied: "Don't defend her. She has never been fond of you and you know it." What could I reply to that? All I said was, "That's true but, still, she must be very hurt." But there was nothing positive to say about her!

Monetary assistance generally flows from the older parent to the adult children, although few old people are able to offer substantial financial help. Direct monetary assistance, rarely exceeding fifty dollars, is less frequent than gift-giving. Gift-giving usually takes the form of monetary contributions for specific articles needed by their children or children's families. In this way the older people contribute indirectly to the maintenance of their children's families.

The older women also play an active role in the observance of special family occasions and holidays. On the days preceding the celebration, they are busy cooking traditional Puerto Rican foods. It is expected that those in good health will participate in the preparation of foods. This is especially true on Christmas and Easter when traditional foods are an essential component of the celebrations.

Cooking for offspring is also a part of everyday life. In many of the households, meals prepared in the Puerto Rican tradition are cooked daily "in case children or grandchildren come by." Josefina Montes, for example, cooks a large quantity of food every day for herself, her husband, and their adult children and grandchildren. Her daughters come by after work to visit and pick up their youngest children, who stay with grandparents after school. The youngest daughter eats dinner at her parents' home. The oldest takes enough food home to serve her family. Doña[3] Josefina's sons frequently drop by after work or during lunch and she always insists that they eat something.

The older women also provide assistance to their children during health crises. When Juana Rivera's son was hospitalized for a hernia operation, she visited the hospital every day, occasionally bringing food she had prepared for him. When her son was released, Doña Juana stayed in his household throughout his convalescence, caring for him while her daughter-in-law went off to work.

The aged women also assist their children by taking care of grandchildren. Grandchildren go to their grandmother's house after school and stay until their parents stop by after work. If the children are not old enough to walk home by themselves, the grandparent waits for them at school and brings them home. The women also take care of their grandchildren when they are not old enough to attend school or are sick. They see their role as grandmothers as a continuation or reenactment of their role as mothers and childrearers.

The women, despite old age, have a place in the functional structure of their families. The older women's assistance is an important contribution to their children's households and also helps validate the women's sense of their importance and helpfulness.

Mutual Assistance in Elderly Couples

Different conceptions of women and men influence interdependence between husband and wife as well as their daily tasks. Older married women are responsible for domestic tasks and perform household chores. They also take care of grandchildren, grocery shopping, and maintaining family relations. Older married men have among their chores depositing Social Security checks, going to the post office, and buying money orders. Although they stay in the house for long periods, the men go out into the community more often than do their wives. They usually stop at the *bodegas*,[4] which serve as a place for socializing and exchange of information, to buy items needed at home and newspapers from Puerto Rico.

Most married couples have a distinctive newspaper reading pattern. The husband comments on the news to his wife as he reads or after he has finished. Sometimes, after her husband finishes reading and commenting on the news, the older woman reads about it herself. Husbands also inform their wives of ongoing neighborhood events learned on their daily stops at the *bodegas*. Wives, on the other hand, inform husbands of familial events learned through their daily telephone conversations and visits from children and other kin members.

The older couple escort each other to service-providing agencies, even though they are usually accompanied by an adult child, adolescent grandchild, or social worker serving as translator. An older man still perceives himself in the role of "family protector" by escorting the women in his family, particularly his wife.

Older husbands and wives provide each other with emotional assistance. They are daily companions and serve as primary sources of confidence for each other, most often sharing children's and grandchildren's problems, health concerns, or financial worries. The couple do not always agree on solutions or approaches for assisting children when sharing their worries about offspring. Many times the woman serves as a mediator in communicating her husband's problems to adult children. The men tend to keep their problems, particularly financial and emotional ones, to themselves or tell their wives but not their children. This behavior rests upon the notion of men as financially responsible for the family, more self-sufficient, and less emotional than women.

Among the older couples, the husband or wife is generally the principal caregiver during the health crises of their spouse. Carmen Ruiz, for example, suffers from chronic anemia and tires easily. Her husband used to be a cook and has taken responsibility for cooking meals and looking after the household. When Providencia Cruz's husband was hospitalized she spent many hours each day at the hospital, wanting to be certain he was comfortable. She brought meals she had cooked for him, arranged his pillows, rubbed him with bay leaf rubbing alcohol, or watched him as he slept. When he was convalescing at home, she was his principal caregiver. Doña Providencia suffers from osteoarthritis and gastric acidity. When she is in pain and spends the day in bed, her husband provides most of the assistance she needs. He goes to the drugstore to buy medicine or ingredients used in folk remedies. He knows how to prepare the mint and chamomile teas she drinks when not feeling well. He also rubs her legs and hands with ointments when the arthritic pain is more intense than usual. Furthermore, during the days that Doña Providencia's ailments last, he performs most of the household chores.

While both spouses live, the couple manages many of their problems on their own. Assistance from other family members with daily chores or help during an illness is less frequent when the woman still lives with her husband than when she lives alone. However, if one or both spouses is ill, help from adult children is more common.

Friends and Neighbors as Community Sources of Support

Friends and neighbors form part of the older women's support network. However, the women differentiate between "neighbors" and "friends." Neighbors, unlike kin and friends, are not an essential component of the network which provides emotional support. They may or may not become friends. Supportive relations with friends involve being instrumental helpers, companions, and confidants. Neighbors are involved only in instrumental help.

Neighbors as Sources of Support

Contact with neighbors takes the form of greetings, occasional visits, and exchanges of food, all of which help to build the basis for reciprocity when and if the need arises. The establishment and maintenance of good relations with neighbors is considered to be important since neighbors are potentially helpful during emergencies or unexpected events. Views such as the following are common: "It is good to get acquainted with your neighbors; you never know when you might need them."

Josefina Rosario, a widow, has lived next door to an older Puerto Rican couple for three years. Exchange of food and occasional visits are part of her interaction with them. Her neighbor's husband, in his mid-sixties, occasionally runs errands for Doña Josefina, who suffers from rheumatoid arthritis and needs a walker to move around. If she runs out of a specific food item, he goes to the grocery store for her. Other times, he buys stamps, mails letters, or goes to the drugstore to pick up some medicines for her. Although Doña Josefina cannot reciprocate in the same way, she repays her neighbors by visiting every other week and exchanging food. Her neighbors tell her she is to call them day or night if she ever feels sick. Although glad to have such "good neighbors" as she call them, she stresses she does not consider them friends and therefore does not confide her personal problems to them.

Supportive Relationships Among Friends

Although friends perform instrumental tasks, the older women believe that a good friend's most important quality is being able to provide emotional support. A friend is someone willing to help during the "good" and "bad" times, and is trustworthy and reserved. Problems may be shared with a friend with the certainty that confidences will not be betrayed. A friend provides emotional support not only during a crisis or problem, but in everyday life. Friends are companions, visiting and/or calling on a regular basis.

Friendship for this group of women is determined along gender lines. They tend to be careful about men. Relationships with males outside the immediate familial group are usually kept at a formal level. Mistrust of men is based upon the women's notion of *machismo*. Since men are conceived of as having a stronger sexual drive, the women are wary of the possibility of sexual advances, either physical or verbal. None of the women regards a male as a confidant friend. Many even emphasize the word *amiga* ("female friend") instead of *amigo* ("male friend"). Remarks such as the following are common:

I've never had an amigo. Men cannot be trusted too much. They might misunderstand your motives and some even try to make a pass at you.

The few times the women refer to a male as a friend they use the term *amigo de la familia* ("friend of the family"). This expression conveys that the friendly relations are not solely between the woman and the man. The expression is generally used to refer to a close friend of the husband. *Amigos de la familia* may perform instrumental tasks, be present at family gatherings and unhappy events, or drop by to chat with the respondent's husband during the day. However, relations are not based on male-female relationships.

Age similarity is another factor that seems to affect selection of friends. The friendship networks of the older women are mainly composed of people sixty years of age and older. Friends who fill the role of confidant are generally women of a similar age. The women believe that younger generations, generally, have little interest in the elders. They also state that people their own age are better able to understand their problems because they share many of the same difficulties and worries.

Friends often serve as escorts, particularly in the case of women who live alone. Those who know some English serve as translators on some occasions. Close friends also help illiterate friends by reading and writing letters.

Most of the support friends provide one another is of an emotional nature, which involves sharing personal problems. Close friends entrust one another with family and health problems. This exchange occurs when friends either visit or call each other on the telephone. A pattern commonly observed between dyads of friends is daily calls. Many women who live alone usually call the friend during the morning hours, to make sure she is all right and to find out how she is feeling.

Another aspect of the emotional support the older women provide one another is daily companionship, occurring more often among those who live alone. For example, Hilda Montes and Rosa Mendoza sit together from 1:00 to 3:00 in the afternoon to watch soap operas and talk about family events, neighborhood happenings, and household management. At 3:00 P.M., whoever is at the other's apartment leaves because their grandchildren usually arrive from school around 4:00 P.M.

Friends are also supportive during health crises. If they cannot come to visit, they inquire daily about their friend's health by telephone. When their health permits, some friends perform menial household chores and always bring food for the sick person. If the occasion requires it, they prepare and/or administer home remedies. Friends, in this sense, alleviate the stress adult children often feel in assisting their aged mothers, particularly those who live by themselves. Friends take turns among themselves or with kin in taking care of the ill during the daytime. Children generally stay throughout the night.

Exchange ties with female friends include instrumental support, companionship, and problem sharing. Friends, particularly age cohorts, play an important role in the emotional well-being of the elders.

The relevance of culture to experience of old age is seen in the influence of value orientations on the expectations these Puerto Rican women have of themselves and those in their informal supportive networks. The way a group's cultural tradition defines and interprets relationships influences how elders use their networks to secure the support needed in old age. At the same time, the extent to which reality fits culturally-based expectations will contribute, to a large extent, to elders' sense of well-being.

Notes

1. The article is based on a nineteen-month ethnographic study. The research was supported by the Danforth Foundation; Sigma Xi; the Scientific Research Society; and the Delta Kappa Gamma Society International.
2. All names are fictitious.
3. The deference term *Doña* followed by the woman's first name is a common way by which to address elderly Puerto Rican women and the one preferred by those who participated in the study.
4. Neighborhood grocery stores, generally owned by Puerto Ricans or other Hispanics, where ethnic foods can be purchased.

References

Barth, F. 1969. Introduction to *Ethnic Groups and Boundaries*, F. Barth, ed. Boston: Little, Brown.

Bastida, E. 1979. "Family Integration and Adjustment to Aging Among Hispanic American Elderly." Ph.D. dissertation, University of Kansas.

Cantor, M. H. 1979. "The Informal Support System of New York's Inner City Elderly: Is Ethnicity a Factor?" In *Ethnicity and Aging*, D. L. Gelfand and A. J. Kutzik, eds. New York: Springer.

Carrasquillo, H. 1982. "Perceived Social Reciprocity and Self-Esteem Among Elderly Barrio Antillean Hispanics and Their Familial Informal Networks." Ph.D. dissertation, Syracuse University.

Delgado, M. 1981. "Hispanic Elderly and Natural Support Systems: A Special Focus on Puerto Ricans." Paper presented at the Scientific Meeting of the Boston Society for Gerontological Psychiatry, November, Boston, Mass.

Donaldson, E. and E. Martinez. 1980. "The Hispanic Elderly of East Harlem." *Aging* 305-306:6-11.

Sánchez-Ayéndez, M. 1984. "Puerto Rican Elderly Women: Aging in an Ethnic Minority Group in the United States." Ph.D. dissertation, University of Massachusetts at Amherst.

Stevens, E. P. 1973. "Marianismo: The Other Face of Machismo in Latin America." In *Female and Male in Latin America*, A. Pescatello, ed. Pittsburgh: University of Pittsburgh Press.

Questions for Reflection

1. What do you think about the concept of "machismo," which "assumes men have a stronger sexual drive than women, need to prove virility by the conquest of women, a dominant position in relation to females, and a belligerent attitude when confronted by male peers"?

2. Similarly, what do you think about the concept of "marianismo," which "presupposes that it is through motherhood that a woman realizes herself and derives her life's greatest satisfactions"?

3. How important are family unity and family interdependence in your family? To what extent does your family exhibit the behaviors that signal family unity and interdependence in Puerto Rican families?

4. Are the sex role expectations held for members of your family similar to those in Puerto Rican families?

5. How do your parents' and grandparents' cultures of origin explain their expectations for you and for other members of your family?

SELECTION NINE

Shawn McDougal (Class of '95), a mathematics major at Williams College who describes himself as "a rootless African-American mongrel from Los Angeles," originally wrote this article as an opinion piece and it was published in the student newspaper. The article challenges us to reconsider what is meant by the term "multicultural" and to question the common practice of equating race with culture. One's cultural background, McDougal suggests, is much more complex than the color of one's skin and it is that complexity that needs to be understood and valued. He cautions us that when we choose to assume false cultural similarities, we stifle the types of interactions that can lead to the level of disclosure that is necessary for relational intimacy.

Mistaken Notions of Multi-culturalism Limit Communication and Self Reflection

Shawn McDougal

I'd like to take a little time to say a few things about multiculturalism. I'm sure (and I hope!) I'll catch flames for some of what I have to say here, but isn't a willingness to expose oneself to vigorous ridicule or criticism a necessary precondition of saying anything valuable or meaningful? Perhaps what I will say here won't be of any real value or meaning for those reading it, but isn't this just another risk of standing to be heard as well?

I've been more and more aware recently of a certain misunderstanding that a lot of people have about culture. People seem to think that race equals culture. A bi (bisexual) friend of mine, who's involved in a romantic relationship with a bi multiracial partner, was remarking recently at how strange and different their relationship was: their relationship was both "multisexual and multicultural." Since I know both people well enough

From *The Williams Record*. Vol. 107, No. 21. p. 3. Reprinted by permission of *The Williams Record* and Shawn McDougal.

to know they do in fact have very different culturo-personal backgrounds, I didn't really challenge my friend's statement. But knowing also that he had used the term "multicultural" solely in reference to his (pure) white raciality, I nodded in agreement, adding that they were "multiracial" as well.

Race does not equal culture. Culture does not equal race. Although they may be correlated, they are not the same, and this confounding of the two is an unfortunate fallacy in our popular thinking about race, identity, and culture that really limits us from having a truly culturally diverse experience with each other. Why is this? Well, first of all, by equating skin-color or facial features with culture, people reduce culture in such a way that real cultural meaning and power is lost. They reduce something that is cumulative, historical, and full of personal meaning and experiences, to something that is arbitrary and superficial (surface—on the face). Although I might have **something** in common with some one who's black, say, because of our similar experiences with racialized consciousness or negative racial stereotyping, etc., that fact alone says virtually nothing about our culture(s). If that person were raised by two white parents in a wealthy suburb, their cultural experience would probably be very different from my own. Likewise if that black person had two parents and a stable home environment, or that person were a child of poor Caribbean immigrants, or what have you. Although we both identify ourselves as 'black,' our cultural experiences could be radically different. The point is that talking about race by itself says very little about culture.

So how do we effectively talk about culture? I alluded to my conception of it above when I used such words as 'cumulative' and 'experiences.' One good way to think about culture—one metaphor—might be as follows: imagine a person's life as being a curve in space, starting at their birth and then twisting about over the days, months, and years of their life, each point on the curve another moment in their experience of living. What a person's culture is can be thought of as, in a sense, the shape their curve has followed, or better, the experiences/forces/people that have given their life-curve its characteristic bends, twists, corners, and overall shape. Following this metaphor, we can see that race is an element in culture only insofar as it serves to provide distinguishing characteristics to a person's life-curve.

An immediate question one should ask is: Who decides what is a distinguishing characteristic of culture and what isn't? Well, that's why I said this is only a metaphor, and not a model. There is no 'objective' measure of some variable called 'cultural difference,' no quantity called the 'cultural gradient' or some other such pseudo-mathematical nonsense.

This question of authority in determining culture points to what I see as an essential aspect of cultural exchange (or multiculturalism), namely, the individual's central role in reflecting on their own life-curves, their own experiences, and using that reflective awareness to think about and communicate with other people. Although we might

be able to make certain educated guesses about Ms. So-and-so's culture, based on our own knowledge of her biography/lifestyle/personality, only Ms. So-and-so has any sort of intimate knowledge of her own experiences, feelings, understanding, influences, etc. The individual is the final arbiter of culture, but culture is by no means arbitrary.

Further, we can see how dynamic culture is. Just because someone's life-curve has had a certain shape or has twisted in a certain direction in the past doesn't mean it will always have that shape or direction. A person can choose to expose themselves to different experiences, and their reflection on these experiences can influence the way their life-curve is shaped in response. We play a role in deciding what matters in our lives. Like a tree shaped by the wind, rain, and sun, as it manifests the code for growth already in its genes, like a river that winds its way in response to its own fluid nature as well as the more or less impermeable nature of the soil, sediment, and rocks; culture is born out of the dialectical relationship between a person's individual awareness and their social circumstances.

What happens when people confuse something like race with culture is a false-culture, a false self-consciousness. People deceive themselves into playing roles—identity games—that don't reflectively and consciously speak to their true culture, their life-curves. They adopt ritualized patterns of behavior and interaction that don't allow any space for honest and open self-reflection. We see the results of this self-deceiving shallowness in the culture of conformity: people adopt the latest fashionable lifestyle(s) uncritically—they just want to fit in. Their culture is the false-culture of whatever happen to be the latest fads. Their thinking is the stereotyped thinking of the herd. They hide their personal-biographical differences behind a facade of uniformity. They end up reducing their unique and problematic selves to easy to swallow (and to stereotype) images: "It's a black thing. . .", "My background is suburban", "I had typical Asian parents. . .", etc. (What the hell are typical Asian parents? Is the 'black thing' of Jamaican immigrants the same as that of transplants from Alabama? Do wealthy suburbanites live like working-class suburbanites?) This reduction of culture to superficial stereotypes facilitates mediated conformity. People can find who they are supposed to be in the simplistic images of identity portrayed in the mass media. (Although the power relations involved in the construction of mass-culture are problematic and not, say, a simple matter of mass mind-control by some elite, it is the case that some few image-makers play a disproportionate role in the establishing of the bounds/terms of cultural-consciousness. Perhaps Big Brother won't come from the government after all, but from the media giants that have such power in deciding what people see, hear, and even think about).

False-culture, or false self-consciousness, doesn't lead to any real cultural exchange for two reasons. First, because people only bring their superficial/stereotypical selves to their general relations with each other, the cultures that end up getting negotiated and 'understood' in their communion/communication are devoid of precisely those gritty, hard-to-reduce, problematic aspects of their personal experience that have shaped them on their profoundest levels.

This discomfort with problematic culture is manifest here at Williams College in the way people tend to stick tightly to groups of people they are most comfortable with (and least challenged by). Social groups here most often seem to be comprised solely of people who already have very similar backgrounds to each other. Further, even if a group is 'multicultural,' it is usually so in exactly the false-culture sort of way: it is made up of people from different backgrounds who submerge any problematic aspects of themselves beneath some stereotyped group identity. People resist talking in depth about their various personal-biographies. It is as if being 'black' or 'Asian' or 'queer' or 'middle class' says it all. If all someone knows how to communicate about their culture is their current life-style, or some stereotypical image of self that they have gathered from their

peer-group, then the whole span of experiences that have shaped them is a closed book. There is nothing to learn from their life. Their life is like a flat image. It may even be pretty, but it is pretty like a picture, divorced from any larger reality. This ahistorical/apersonal approach to culture is virtually useless for any real exchange of information between people.

The second reason that false-culture inhibits cultural exchange follows from the subjective-experiential nature of culture: for an individual to communicate his or her culture requires that he or she has some reflective awareness of how his or her life has been shaped. Someone who doesn't reflect on their experiences can't communicate those experiences to other people.

In short: Although I might meet someone who has a radically different background than my own, unless we talk about more than our favorite sports teams or current love-interests, there is no real cultural exchange going on. And if we only think about the present and the future, and we don't reflectively think about our pasts, any cultural exchange is empty and false. Any 'multiculturalism' based on false and simplistic notions of culture is not multiculturalism at all, but some convenient and ultimately valueless substitute.

Questions for Reflection

1. What false cultural groups do you have the tendency to associate yourself with?

2. What are the distinct cultural groups that have shaped your life curve to this point?

3. Discuss one relationship that you have with someone "radically different from you" that could become more meaningful if you were to risk talking about something more than superficial topics. What prevents you from doing this?

SELECTION TEN

The previous article used the metaphor that one's personal culture is the shape that their personal curve has followed in space. The article suggested that it is overly simplistic to assume that one "knows" to what cultural group another person belongs. Such assumptions can lead to all sorts of communication and relationship difficulties. In this article Sucheng Chan, Professor of History and Chair of the Asian American Studies Program at the University of California, Santa Barbara, sketches for us the shape her own curve has followed. Dr. Chan illustrates how she has been actively involved in determining that shape. Your text discusses how self-fulfilling prophesies affect self-esteem and self-image. Note the effects that various "prophecies" had on this author.

You're Short, Besides!

Sucheng Chan

When asked to write about being a physically handicapped Asian American woman, I considered it an insult. After all, my accomplishments are many, yet I was not asked to write about any of them. Is being handicapped the most salient feature about me? The fact that it might be in the eyes of others made me decide to write the essay as requested. I realized that the way I think about myself may differ considerably from the way others perceive me. And maybe that's what being physically handicapped is all about.

I was stricken simultaneously with pneumonia and polio at the age of four. Uncertain whether I had polio of the lungs, seven of the eight doctors who attended me—all practitioners of Western medicine—told my parents they should not feel optimistic about my survival. A Chinese fortune teller my mother consulted also gave a grim prog-

nosis, but for an entirely different reason: I had been stricken because my name was offensive to the gods. My grandmother had named me "grandchild of wisdom," a name that the fortune teller said was too presumptuous for a girl. So he advised my parents to change my name to "chaste virgin." All these pessimistic predictions notwithstanding, I hung onto life, if only by a thread. For three years, my body was periodically pierced with electric shocks as the muscles of my legs atrophied. Before my illness, I had been an active, rambunctious, precocious, and very curious child. Being confined to bed was thus a mental agony as great as my physical pain. Living in war-torn China, I received little medical attention; physical therapy was unheard of. But I was determined to walk. So one day, when I was six or seven, I instructed my mother to set up two rows of chairs to face each other so that I could use them as I would parallel bars. I attempted to walk by holding my body up and moving it forward with my arms while dragging my legs along behind. Each time I fell, my mother gasped, but I

From *Making Waves* by Asian Women United. ©1989 by Asian Women United. Reprinted by permission of Beacon Press.

badgered her until she let me try again. After four nonambulatory years, I finally walked once more by pressing my hands against my thighs so my knees wouldn't buckle.

My father had been away from home during most of those years because of the war. When he returned, I had to confront the guilt he felt about my condition. In many East Asian cultures, there is a strong folk belief that a person's physical state in this life is a reflection of how morally or sinfully he or she lived in previous lives. Furthermore, because of the tendency to view the family as a single unit, it is believed that the fate of one member can be caused by the behavior of another. Some of my father's relatives told him that my illness had doubtless been caused by the wild carousing he did in his youth. A well-meaning but somewhat simple man, my father believed them.

Throughout my childhood, he sometimes apologized to me for having to suffer retribution for his former bad behavior. This upset me; it was bad enough that I had to deal with the anguish of not being able to walk, but to have to assuage his guilt as well was a real burden! In other ways, my father was very good to me. He took me out often, carrying me on his shoulders or back, to give me fresh air and sunshine. He did this until I was too large and heavy for him to carry. And ever since I can remember, he has told me that I am pretty.

After getting over her anxieties about my constant falls, my mother decided to send me to school. I had already learned to read some words of Chinese at the age of three by asking my parents to teach me the sounds and meaning of various characters in the daily newspaper. But between the ages of four and eight, I received no education since just staying alive was a full-time job. Much to her chagrin, my mother found no school in Shanghai, where we lived at the time, which would accept me as a student. Finally, as a last resort, she approached the American School which agreed to enroll me only if my family kept an *amah* (a servant who takes care of children) by my side at all times. The tuition at the school was twenty U.S. dollars per month—a huge sum of money during those years of runaway inflation in China—and payable only in U.S. dollars. My family afforded the high cost of tuition and the expense of employing a full-time *amah* for less than a year.

We left China as the Communist forces swept across the country in victory. We found an apartment in Hong Kong across the street from a school run by Seventh-Day Adventists. By that time I could walk a little, so the principal was persuaded to accept me. An *amah* now had to take care of me only during recess when my classmates might easily knock me over as they ran about the playground.

After a year and a half in Hong Kong, we moved to Malaysia, where my father's family had lived for four generations. There I learned to swim in the lovely warm waters of the tropics and fell in love with the sea. On land I was a cripple; in the ocean I could move with the grace of a fish. I liked the freedom of being in the water so much that many years later, when I was a graduate student in Hawaii, I became greatly enamored with a man just because he called me a "Polynesian water nymph."

As my overall health improved, my mother became less anxious about all aspects of my life. She did everything possible to enable me to lead as normal a life as possible. I remember how once some of her colleagues in the high school where she taught criticized her for letting me wear short skirts. They felt my legs should not be exposed to public view. My mother's response was, "All girls her age wear short skirts, so why shouldn't she?"

The years in Malaysia were the happiest of my childhood, even though I was constantly fending off children who ran after me calling, *"Baikah! Baikah!"* ("Cripple! Cripple!" in the Hokkien dialect commonly spoken in Malaysia). The taunts of children mattered little because I was a star pupil. I won one award after another for general scholarship as well as for art and public speaking. Whenever the school had important visitors my teacher always called on me to recite in front of the class.

A significant event that marked me indelibly occurred when I was twelve. That year my school held a music recital and I was one of the students chosen to play the piano. I managed to get up the steps to the stage without any problem, but as I walked across the stage, I fell. Out of the audience, a voice said loudly and clearly, "Ayah! A *baikah* shouldn't be allowed to perform in public." I got up before anyone could get on stage to help me and, with tears streaming uncontrollably down my face, I rushed to the piano and began to play. Beethoven's "Fur Elise" had never been played so fiendishly fast before or since, but I managed to finish the whole piece. That I managed to do so made me feel really strong. I never again feared ridicule.

In later years I was reminded of this experience from time to time. During my fourth year as an assistant professor at the University of California at Berkeley, I won a distinguished teaching award. Some weeks later I ran into a former professor who congratulated me enthusiastically. But I said to him, "You know what? I became a distinguished teacher by *limping* across the stage of Dwinelle 155!" (Dwinelle 155 is a large, cold classroom that most colleagues of mine hate to teach in.) I was rude not because I lacked graciousness but because this man, who had told me that my dissertation was the finest piece of work he had read in fifteen years, had nevertheless advised me to eschew a teaching career.

"Why?" I asked.

"Your leg . . ." he responded.

"What about my leg?" I said, puzzled.

"Well, how would you feel standing in front of a large lecture class?"

"If it makes any difference, I want you to know I've won a number of speech contests in my life, and I am not the least bit self-conscious about speaking in front of large audiences. . . . Look, why don't you write me a letter of recommendation to tell people how brilliant I am, and let *me* worry about my leg!"

This incident is worth recounting only because it illustrates a dilemma that handicapped persons face frequently: those who care about us sometimes get so protective that they unwittingly limit our growth. This former professor of mine had been one of my greatest supporters for two decades. Time after time, he had written glowing letters of recommendation on my behalf. He had spoken as he did because he thought he had my best interests at heart; he thought that if I got a desk job rather than one that required me to be a visible, public person, I would be spared the misery of being stared at.

Americans, for the most part, do not believe as Asians do that physically handicapped persons are morally flawed. But they are equally inept at interacting with those of us who are not able-bodied. Cultural differences in the perception and treatment of handicapped people are most clearly expressed by adults. Children, regardless of where they are, tend to be openly curious about people who do not look "normal." Adults in Asia have no hesitation in asking visibly handicapped people what is wrong with them, often expressing their sympathy with looks of pity, whereas adults in the United States try desperately to be polite by pretending not to notice.

One interesting response I often elicited from people in Asia but have never encountered in America is the attempt to link my physical condition to the state of my soul. Many a time while living and traveling in Asia people would ask me what religion I belonged to. I would tell them that my mother is a devout Buddhist, that my father was baptized a Catholic but has never practiced Catholicism, and that I am an agnostic. Upon hearing this, people would try strenuously to convert me to their religion so that whichever God they believed in could bless me. If I would only attend this church or that temple regularly, they urged, I would surely get cured. Catholics and Buddhists alike have pressed religious medallions into my palm, telling me if I would wear these, the relevant deity or saint would make me well. Once while visiting the tomb of Muhammad Ali Jinnah in Karachi, Pakistan, an old Muslim, after finishing his evening prayers, spotted me, gestured toward my legs, raised his arms heavenward, and began a new round of prayers, apparently on my behalf.

In the United States adults who try to act "civilized" towards handicapped people by pretending they don't notice anything unusual sometimes end up ignoring handicapped people completely. In the first few months I lived in this country, I was struck by the fact that whenever children asked me what was the matter with my leg, their adult companions would hurriedly shush them up, furtively look at me, mumble apologies, and rush their children away. After a few months of such encounters, I decided it was my responsibility to educate these people. So I would say to the flustered adults, "It's okay, let the kid ask." Turning to the child, I would say, "When I was a little girl, no bigger than you are, I became sick with something called polio. The muscles in my leg shrank up and I couldn't walk very well. You're much luckier than I am because now you can get a vaccine to make sure you never get my disease. So don't cry when your mommy takes you to get a polio vaccine, okay?" Some adults and their little companions I talked to this way were glad to be rescued from embarrassment; others thought I was strange.

Americans have another way of covering up their uneasiness: they become jovially patronizing. Sometimes when people spot my crutch, they ask if I've had a skiing accident. When I answer that unfortunately it is something less glamorous than that, they say, "I bet you *could* ski if you put your mind to it!" Alternately, at parties where people dance, men who ask me to dance with them get almost belligerent when I decline their invitation. They say, "Of course you can dance if you *want* to!" Some have given me pep talks about how if I would only develop the right mental attitude, I would have more fun in life.

Different cultural attitudes toward handicapped persons came out clearly during my wedding. My father-in-law, as solid a representative of middle America as could be found, had no qualms about objecting to the marriage on racial

grounds, but he could bring himself to comment on my handicap only indirectly. He wondered why his son, who had dated numerous high school and college beauty queens, couldn't marry one of them instead of me. My mother-in-law, a devout Christian, did not share her husband's prejudices, but she worried aloud about whether I could have children. Some Chinese friends of my parents, on the other hand, said that I was lucky to have found such a noble man, one who would marry me despite my handicap. I, for my part, appeared in church in a white lace wedding dress I had designed and made myself—a miniskirt!

How Asian Americans treat me with respect to my handicap tells me a great deal about their degree of acculturation. Recent immigrants behave just like Asians in Asia; those who have been here longer or who grew up in the United States behave more like their white counterparts. I have not encountered any distinctly Asian American pattern of response. What makes the experience of Asian American handicapped people unique is the duality of responses we elicit.

Regardless of racial or cultural background, most handicapped people have to learn to find a balance between the desire to attain physical independence and the need to take care of ourselves by not overtaxing our bodies. In my case, I've had to learn to accept the fact that leading an active life has its price. Between the ages of eight and eighteen, I walked without using crutches or braces but the effort caused my right leg to become badly misaligned. Soon after I came to the United States, I had a series of operations to straighten out the bones of my right leg; afterwards though my leg looked straighter and presumably better, I could no longer walk on my own. Initially my doctors fitted me with a brace, but I found wearing one cumbersome and soon gave it up. I could move around much more easily—and more important, faster—by using one crutch. One orthopedist after another warned me that using a single crutch was a bad practice. They were right. Over the years my spine developed a double-S curve and for the last twenty years I have suffered from severe, chronic back pains, which neither conventional physical therapy nor a lighter work load can eliminate.

The only thing that helps my backaches is a good massage, but the soothing effect lasts no more than a day or two. Massages are expensive, especially when one needs them three times a week. So I found a job that pays better, but at which I have to work longer hours, consequently increasing the physical strain on my body—a sort of vicious circle. When I was in my thirties, my doctors told me that if I kept leading the strenuous life I did, I would be in a wheelchair by the time I was forty. They were right on target: I bought myself a wheelchair when I was forty-one. But being the incorrigible character that I am, I use it only when I am *not* in a hurry!

It is a good thing, however, that I am too busy to think much about my handicap or my backaches because pain can physically debilitate as well as cause depression. And there are days when my spirits get rather low. What has helped me is realizing that being handicapped is akin to growing old at an accelerated rate. The contradiction I experience is that often my mind races along as though I'm only twenty while my body feels about sixty. But fifteen or twenty years hence, unlike my peers who will have to cope with aging for the first time, I shall be full of cheer because I will have already fought, and I hope won, that battle long ago.

Beyond learning how to be physically independent and, for some of us, living with chronic pain or other kinds of discomfort, the most difficult thing a handicapped person has to deal with, especially during puberty and early adulthood, is relating to potential sexual partners. Because American culture places so much emphasis on physical attractiveness, a person with a shriveled limb, or a tilt to the head, or the inability to speak clearly, experiences great uncertainty—indeed trauma—when interacting with someone to whom he or she is attracted. My problem was that I was not only physically handicapped, small, and

short, but worse, I also wore glasses and was smarter than all the boys I knew! Alas, an insurmountable combination. Yet somehow I have managed to have intimate relationships, all of them with extraordinary men. Not surprisingly, there have also been countless men who broke my heart—men who enjoyed my company "as a friend," but who never found the courage to date or make love with me, although I am sure my experience in this regard is no different from that of many able-bodied persons.

The day came when my backaches got in the way of having an active sex life. Surprisingly that development was liberating because I stopped worrying about being attractive to men. No matter how headstrong I had been, I, like most women of my generation, had had the desire to be alluring to men ingrained into me. And that longing had always worked like a brake on my behavior. When what men think of me ceased to be compelling, I gained greater freedom to be myself.

I've often wondered if I would have been a different person had I not been physically handicapped. I really don't know, though there is no question that being handicapped has marked me. But at the same time I usually do not *feel* handicapped—and consequently, I do not *act* handicapped. People are therefore less likely to treat me as a handicapped person. There is no doubt, however, that the lives of my parents, sister, husband, other family members, and some close friends have been affected by my physical condition. They have had to learn not to hide me away at home, not to feel embarrassed by how I look or react to people who say silly things to me, and not to resent me for the extra demands my condition makes on them. Perhaps the hardest thing for those who live with handicapped people is to know when and how to offer help. There are no guidelines applicable to all situations. My advice is, when in doubt, ask, but ask, in a way that does not smack of pity or embarrassment. Most important, please don't talk to us as though we are children.

So, has being physically handicapped been a handicap? It all depends on one's attitude. Some years ago, I told a friend that I had once said to an affirmative action compliance officer (somewhat sardonically since I do not believe in the head count approach to affirmative action) that the institution which employs me is triply lucky because it can count me as nonwhite, female and handicapped. He responded, "Why don't you tell them to count you four times? . . . Remember, you're short, besides!"

Questions for Reflection

1. Describe the emotional reactions you had while reading this article. Why do you suppose you reacted this way?
2. Analyze how the concept of self-fulfilling prophesy applies to Dr. Chan. What lessons do you learn from this analysis?

SELECTION ELEVEN

The shape of our personal curve is mediated by many events and interactions with countless people, some of whom we do not even "know." In this article, which was published just as Karen K. Russell graduated from Harvard Law School, Ms. Russell does not hide behind false cultural labels, but instead allows us to "know" her and to share in some of the memorable communication encounters that helped to give shape to her curve. The textbook describes the important skill of empathizing. As you read this article, note the intensity and character of your empathic reactions.

Growing Up with Privilege and Prejudice

Karen K. Russell

To our children . . . in the hope that they will grow up as we could not . . . equal . . . and understanding.
    William Felton Russell,
    William Frances McSweeny

In 1966, my father and his co-author dedicated his first autobiography, "Go Up for Glory." Today, in 1987, having just received my Doctor of Laws degree, I wonder if I can fulfill the dreams of my parents' generation. They struggled for integration, they marched for peace, they "sat in" for equality. I doubt they were naive enough to think they had changed the world, but I know they hoped my generation would be able to approach life differently. In fact, we have been able to do things my parents never thought possible. But that is not enough.

I am a child of privilege. In so many ways, I have been given every opportunity—good grade schools, college years at Georgetown, the encouragement to pursue my ambitions. I have just graduated from Harvard Law School. My future looks promising. Some people, no doubt, will attribute any successes I have to the fact that I am a black woman. I am a child of privilege, and I am angry.

In "The Book of Laughter and Forgetting," Milan Kundera writes: "The struggle of man against power is the struggle of memory against forgetting." It seems that we have not come very far in that struggle in this country. We have entered the post-civil rights, post-feminist era, both movements I owe so much to. Meanwhile, my parents' dreams are still around us, still unrealized.

It is perhaps somewhat ironic that I came back for my postgraduate work to Boston, a city my father once described as the most racist in America. My father is Bill Russell, center for the Boston Celtics dynasty that won 11 championships in 13 years. Recently, I asked him if it was difficult to send me to school here. When he first went to Boston in 1956, the Celtics' only black player, fans and sportswriters subjected him to the worst kind of unbridled bigotry. When he retired from the National Basketball Association in 1969, he moved to the West Coast where he has remained.

I found his response to my question surprising. "I played for the Celtics, period," he said. "I did not play for Boston. I was able to separate the

From *New York Times Magazine* 136 (June 14, 1987): 69–74. ©1987 by The New York Times Company. Reprinted by permission.

Celtics institution from the city and the fans. When I sent you to Harvard, I expected you to be able to do the same. I wanted you to have the best possible education and to be able to make the best contacts. I knew you'd encounter racism and sexism, and maybe, in some ways that's a good thing. If you were too sheltered, I'm afraid you'd be too naive. If you were too sheltered, you might not be motivated to help others who do not have your advantages."

Looking back on my tenure at Harvard, I guess he was right; the last three years have opened my eyes, but law school was only part of it. I became much more aware of disparities in wealth, gender, status. The race issue had always been with me, but it hadn't occurred to me that my generation would still be saddled with so many other limitations.

Actually, people of my generation have a new breed of racism (and sexism and classism) to contend with. The new racism is more subtle, and in some ways more difficult to confront. Open bigotry is out, but there have been a number of overtly racist incidents recently, at Howard Beach in New York, for example, and on college campuses throughout the country. What provokes these incidents? The new racism seems to be partially submerged, coming out into the open when sparked by a sudden confrontation. Then there is the sort of comment Al Campanis, then a Los Angeles Dodgers vice president, made recently on the ABC News program "Nightline," that blacks "may not have some of the necessities" required to achieve leadership positions in baseball. Campanis continued that lacking necessities could be demonstrated in other areas: blacks are not good swimmers, he said, "because they don't have the buoyancy." (I've already ordered my "I'm Black and I'm Buoyant" bumper sticker.)

The Campanis incident is more than just your garden-variety, knee-jerk racism. I sincerely doubt that Campanis meant any harm to come from his remarks; in fact, he probably doesn't think of himself as a racist. But does it matter? How am I supposed to react to well-meaning, good, liberal white people who say things like: "You know, Karen, I don't understand what all the fuss is about. You're one of my good friends, and I never think of you as black." Implicit in such a remark is, "I think of you as white," or perhaps just, "I don't think of your race at all." Racial neutrality is a wonderful concept, but we are a long way from achieving it. In the meantime, I would hope that people wouldn't have to negate my race in order to accept me.

Last year, I worked as a summer law associate, and one day a white lawyer called me into her office. She told me, laughing, that her secretary, a young black woman, had said that I spoke "more white than white people." It made me sad; that young woman had internalized all of society's negative images of black people to the point that she thought of a person with clear diction as one of "them."

I am reminded of the time during college that I was looking through the classifieds for an apartment. I called a woman to discuss the details of a rental. I needed directions to the apartment, and she asked me where I lived. I told her I lived in Georgetown, to which she replied, "Can you believe the way the blacks have overrun Georgetown?" I didn't really know how to respond. I said, "Well, actually, I can believe that Georgetown is filled with blacks because I happen to be black." There was a silence on the other end. Finally, the woman tried to explain that she hadn't meant any harm. She was incredibly embarrassed, and, yes, you guessed it, she said, "Some of my best friends are. . . ." I hung up before she could finish.

I was afraid to come back to Boston. My first memory of the place is of a day spent in Marblehead, walking along the ocean shore with a white friend of my parents. I must have been 3 or 4 years old. A white man walking past us looked at me and said, "You little nigger." I am told that I smiled up at him as he went on: "They should send all you black baboons back to Africa." It was only when I turned to look at Kay that I realized something was wrong.

We lived in a predominantly Irish Catholic neighborhood in Reading, Mass. For a long time, we were the only black family there. It was weird to be the only black kid at school, aside from my two older brothers. I knew we were different from the other children. Notwithstanding that, I loved school. In 1968, in the first grade, we held mock Presidential elections, and the teacher kept a tally on the blackboard as she counted ballots. There were 20 votes for Hubert H. Humphrey, four or five votes for Richard M. Nixon and one vote for Dick Gregory. No one else in the classroom had heard of Gregory. I was mortified. But I had just done what the other kids had done: I had voted like my parents.

I think my brothers and I may have been spared some of the effects of racism because my father was a celebrity. But I know that his position also made us a bit paranoid. Sometimes it was hard to tell why other kids liked us, or hated us, for that matter. Was it because we had a famous father? Was it because we were black? We had one of those "fun" houses—lots of food, lots of toys, and, the coup de grace, a swimming pool. I was proud to have friends over. They were awed by my father's trophy case. Actually, so were we.

One night we came home from a three-day weekend and found we had been robbed. Our house was in a shambles, and "NIGGA" was spray-painted on the walls. The burglars had poured beer on the pool table and ripped up the felt. They had broken into my father's trophy case and smashed most of the trophies. I was petrified and shocked at the mess; everyone was very upset. The police came, and after a while, they left. It was then that my parents pulled back their bedcovers to discover that the burglars had defecated in their bed.

Every time the Celtics went out on the road, vandals would come and tip over our garbage cans. My father went to the police station to complain. The police told him that raccoons were responsible, so he asked where he could apply for a gun permit. The raccoons never came back.

The only time we were *really* scared was after my father wrote an article about racism in professional basketball for The Saturday Evening Post. He earned the nickname Felton X. We received threatening letters, and my parents notified the Federal Bureau of Investigation. What I find most telling about this episode is that years later, after Congress had passed the Freedom of Information Act, my father requested his F.B.I. file and found that he was repeatedly referred to therein as "an arrogant Negro who won't sign autographs for white children."

My father has never given autographs, because he thinks they are impersonal. He would rather shake a person's hand or look that person in the eye and say, "Pleased to meet you." His attitude has provoked racist responses, and these have tended to obscure the very basic issue of the right to privacy. Any professional athlete, and certainly any black professional athlete, is supposed to feel grateful to others for the fame he or she has achieved. The thoughtless interruptions, the insistence by fans that they be recognized and personally thanked for their support, never let up. I'll never forget the day I left for college at Georgetown. I had never been away from either parent for more than two weeks, and now I was moving 3,000 miles away. I was at the airport, saying goodbye to my friends and my family. I was crying so hard that I actually cried my contact lens out. And I was hugging my dad—it was a real Hallmark moment. A man came up, oblivious to the gathering, and said to him, "You're Wilt Chamberlain, aren't you?" We all turned to look at him as though he were crazy. He asked for an autograph. My father declined.

I always admired the way my father dealt with these intrusions. He never compromised his values. It would have been easier to acquiesce to the fans—or to a sponsor who offered him a lower fee than they would a white person for endorsing a product. But he would not. I struggle to emulate him.

I went to college with Patrick Ewing, whose playing style has been compared to my father's.

Patrick came to Georgetown from the public high school in Cambridge, just a few blocks from the Harvard campus. I have a lot of sympathy for him. When he played in college, people in the stands—presumably educated people—held up signs that said "Patrick Ewing Can't Read Dis."

When my father first played for the Celtics, the fans called him "chocolate boy," "coon," "nigger,"—you name it, he was called it. Almost three decades later, Patrick Ewing was facing the same sort of treatment, and I was, in a way, reliving my father's experience in watching it happen. I never talked to Patrick about it because I respected his privacy. From being in public with my father, I knew how difficult it was to be someone like Patrick. Aside from everything else, when you're over 6 feet, 9 inches tall—as both of them are—it's hard to be inconspicuous. Your presence seems to make other people uncomfortable, and everyone seems to feel further compelled to speak to you. Still, I hoped Patrick knew he wasn't alone.

Several weeks ago, I heard on the news about a racial incident in Taunton, a town not far from Cambridge. It concerned two girls, high-school students and best friends. One was black, the other white. When the school yearbook arrived, it was discovered that the caption under the photograph of the white girl included the words "Nigger Lover." On the news, the school principal said that the incident was just an isolated "prank," not a racist act.

I remember a day in my own high school when a guy who was really popular walked by me in the hall and hissed "nigger" under his breath. I told one of my close friends, and she insisted that I must have misunderstood him, that he must have said "bigger." I felt betrayed.

I feel awful for those girls in Taunton. Adolescents can be really cruel. Adults may have the same thoughts, but they are not as likely to say them to your face. Not that the latter is necessarily an improvement. I could always pinpoint the source of the bigotry in my high school, but the new bigot is much harder to detect. Our society has taken to the presumption that racism—and

sexism—no longer exist, and that any confrontations are the work of a few "bad actors." Given this myth, the person who complains about genuine harassment can expect to be seen as the source of conflict.

In Taunton, they crossed out the epithet in every copy of the yearbook. It would apparently have been too expensive to recall the edition. Too expensive for whom? . . .

My friends, from Harvard and elsewhere, reflect my fragmented background. I could never invite them all to the same party and survive. Nor can I meet them all on the same ground. At the law school, I made friends with fellow anti-apartheid protesters and members of a loose-knit group of leftists known as the counterhegemonic front. I have other friends whose politics I strongly disagree with. I have sometimes been drawn to the children of famous or wealthy parents because of an immediate sense of commonality; we know how to protect one another. One of my best friends is Chris Kennedy, son of Ethel and the late Robert F. Kennedy. We never use last names when introducing each other, because we resent people who remember only our last names. . . .

How will I deal with racism in my life? I have no brilliant solution. On a personal level, I will ask people to explain a particular comment or joke. When I have trouble hailing a cab in New York, as frequently happens—cabbies "don't want to go to Harlem"—I will copy down the medallion numbers and file complaints if necessary. On the larger level, I will work with others to confront the dilemma of the widening gap between the black middle class and the black lower class, a gap that must be closed if my generation is to advance the cause of racial equality.

Like many middle-class children who grew up accustomed to a comfortable life style, I will also have to work to balance the desire for economic prosperity with the desire to realize more idealistic goals.

If I do ever find a man and get married (after all those magazine and newspaper articles, I realize that I have a better chance of becoming a member of the Politburo!), will we want to raise our kids in a black environment? Sometimes I really regret that I didn't go to an all-black college. When I was in high school on Mercer Island, I didn't go out on dates. A good friend was nice enough to escort me to my senior prom. I don't know if I want my kids excluded like that. If it hadn't been my race, it might have been something else; I guess a lot of people were miserable in high school. Yet, I have to wonder what it would be like to be the norm.

I am concerned about tokenism. If I am successful, I do not want to be used as a weapon to defeat the claims of blacks who did not have my opportunities. I do not want someone to say of me: "See, she made it. We live in a world of equal opportunity. If you don't make it, it's your own fault."

I also worry about fallout from this article. One day during college, I was walking down the street when a photographer asked if he could take my picture for the Style section of The Washington Post. The photograph appeared with a caption that said I worked at a modeling agency, which I did—as a booking agent. Two things happened. I got asked out on some dates, which I didn't mind. And I received a letter that, accompanied by detailed anatomical description, said I was "a nigger bitch who has no business displaying your ugly body." What kind of letters and comments can I expect to receive as a result of this article? Although I am speaking as an individual, I run the risk of being depersonalized, even dehumanized, by others.

Daddy told me that he never listened to the boos because he never listened to the cheers. He did it for himself. I guess I have to, too.

Question for Reflection

1. Describe an incident in which a person used a racist or sexist label to describe you. How did you feel? Do you always feel that way when someone labels you thus? If not, what about the context or relationship causes you to have a different reaction?

SELECTION TWELVE

Before you read this poem, go back to the introduction to this text and re-read the opening poem by Paul Laurence Dunbar. This poem by Elisa Martinez, an elementary school teacher of severely disabled children and former director of Teatro de los Pobres, was written in Spanish, but the power of its message in explaining the importance and advantages of recognizing and celebrating diversity within each of us comes through clearly in this English translation.

Having the Choice of Who to Be

Elisa Martinez

As Mexican Americans, we are often criticized for not flowing in the mainstream of America. Why do "they" insist on speaking "that language" and retaining "that" culture when "they" live in the United States?

I can't answer that question for anyone else. But as for me, I find that it makes life more interesting.

By all appearances, I am one person but in reality I am two.

It is one of me who cries when she hears melancholy memories of mother and father; it is the other who sighs when she hears "Goodnight Sweetheart," with her memories of friends, proms and malts at the drive-in.

It is one of me who enjoys a slice of medium rare roast beef and the other who wraps it in a tortilla and downs it with hot chili sauce.

It is one of me who jerks in rhythm to "Billie Jean" and the other who swirls gaily to corridos[1] and steps in rhythm to a cumbia.[2]

It is one of me who prepares for Santa Claus and the other who breaks the piñata at the Posada.[3]

It is one of me who wants to be always on time and the other who gets there just a little bit late.

It is one of me who interprets Serafina in Tennessee Williams' "Rose Tattoo" and the other who becomes "La Siempreviva" in Luis Basurto's "Cada Quién Su Vida."[4]

From *Chiquita's Cocoon*, by Bettina R. Flores (New York, NY: Villard Books, 1994) 27–30. Translated by Bettina R. Flores. Reprinted by permission of Villard Books.

[1] A Mexican polka.
[2] A salsa-type dance.
[3] A twelve-day Christmas celebration.
[4] La Siempreviva is the leading lady in "Cada Quién Su Vida" ("To Each His Own").

It is one of me who carves out the face in the pumpkin for Halloween and the other who cleans the sepulcro[5] on Día de Los Muertos.[6]

It is one of me who buys the smoke alarm for the safety of the family and the other who has it disconnected when it drives us mad every time a tortilla burns.

It is one of me who buys medication at the drugstore and the other who washes it down with estafiate.[7]

It is one of me who can appreciate Beverly Sills in concert and the other me who can appreciate "The Poet and Peasant Overture" played beautifully by a group of mariachis.[8]

It is one of me who takes great pains to speak English correctly, giving great care to the rules of grammar, and the other *me* who say says Qué cute![9] and Simón que yes![10]

It is one of me who celebrates Mother's Day on the second Sunday in May and other *me* who celebrates again on May 10.

It is one of me who feels the patriotic emotion when the Stars and Stripes go by and the other who elates at the tri-colored flag with the eagle in the center as she marches by to the rhythm of the bugles.

The other day as I was cleaning house, I was singing that popular Nelson/Iglesias release "To All the Girls I Loved Before." My husband, who incidentally does not appreciate my singing

(another Mexican custom), asked, "And who are you, Willie or Julio?"

How neat, I thought, that I DO have a choice.

Questions for Reflection

1. What are the choices that you have about who to be?
2. Can you identify the ways in which the "mixes" of your own cultural heritage play themselves out in the decisions and behaviors of your everyday life?
3. What are your personal reactions to both the Paul Laurence Dunbar poem which began this book and this poem?

---

[5] A grave.
[6] Day of the Dead.
[7] A Mexican tea used for health purposes.
[8] A group of musicians.
[9] How cute!
[10] Of course!